£8.99

The Official FA Guide to
Basic Refereeing

LEARNING

The Official FA Guide to
Basic Refereeing

John Baker
Head of Refereeing, The FA

Hodder & Stoughton

A MEMBER OF THE HODDER HEADLINE GROUP

For order enquiries: please contact Bookpoint Ltd, 130 Milton Park, Abingdon, Oxon OX14 4SB. Telephone: +44 (0) 1235 827720. Fax: +44 (0) 1235 400454. Lines are open from 09.00–18.00, Monday to Saturday with a 24-hour message-answering service. Details about our titles and how to order are available at www.madaboutbooks.com

British Library Cataloguing in Publication Data:
a catalogue record for this title is available from the British Library.

ISBN 0 340 81604 X

First Published 2004
Impression number   10 9 8 7 6 5 4 3 2
Year   2007 2006 2005 2004

Managing Editor: Jonathan Wilson, FA Learning

Typeset by Servis Filmsetting Ltd, Manchester.
Printed in Great Britain for Hodder & Stoughton Educational, a division of Hodder Headline Plc, 338 Euston Road, London NW1 3BH by Cox & Wyman, Reading, Berkshire.

Hodder Headline's policy is to use papers that are natural, renewable and recyclable products and made from wood grown in sustainable forests. The logging and manufacturing processes are expected to conform to the environmental regulations of the country of origin.

Contents

LEARNING

Philosophy of the guides

The aim of these **Official FA Guides** is to reach the millions of people who participate in football or who are involved in the game in other ways – at any level.

Each book aims to increase your awareness and understanding of association football and in this understanding to enhance, increase, improve and extend your involvement in the world's greatest game.

These books are designed to be interactive and encourage you to apply what you read and to help you to translate this knowledge into practical skills and ability. Specific features occur throughout this book to assist this process:

■ Tasks will appear in this form and will make you think about what you have just learned and how you will apply it in a practical way.

Best Practice The Best Practice feature will give you an example of a good or ideal way of doing things – this could be on or off the pitch.

| Quote | 'Quotes throughout will pass on useful knowledge or insight or encourage you to consider a certain aspect of your skills or responsibilities.' |

Statistic

The statistics included will often surprise and will certainly increase your knowledge of the game.

Summary

* **The summaries at the end of each chapter will recap on its contents and help you to consolidate your knowledge and understanding.**

You can read this guide in any way you choose and prefer to do so – at home, on the pitch, in its entirety, or to dip in for particular advice. Whatever way you use it, we hope it increases your ability, your knowledge, your involvement, and most importantly your enjoyment and passion to **be a part of the game**.

Introduction

All the fans I know or come across at matches think that they can do as good a job as the referee. They have often been involved in football for much of their lives and firmly believe that they understand the Laws of Association Football. To a certain extent this is clearly true, although this book will highlight certain misunderstandings of the Laws which have been passed from father to son and from player to player.

The introductory paragraph presents me with a need to explain the use of the male pronoun throughout this book. In recognition of the massive increase in popularity of the women's game and the 100% increase in the number of female match officials I decided to modify the text in draft two of the book to replace 'he' with 'he/she', etc. Unfortunately, the text became so cumbersome that I have decided to follow convention and include the following statement produced in all Federation of International Football Associations (FIFA) and The Football Association (The FA) documents:

Quote | 'References to the male gender in this publication in respect of referees, assistant referees, players and officials are for simplification and apply to both males and females.'

Everyone claims to fully understand the Laws of the Game but as soon as we make an assessment of that knowledge through questions based on match situations, we often find that knowledge inadequate.

Referees need to know the Laws and be able to recognize incidents. This book will help all readers to appreciate the referee's job.

Referees can only give decisions on what they see. Your view from the sideline, the stand or the comfort of your lounge with pictures from any of the cameras the director chooses may be very different from that of the referee on the pitch. Players getting in the way, the ball breaking from one end to the other in a counter attack, events happening on the blind side of the referee all conspire to challenge the referee's view. Being aware of patterns of play and the behaviour of players enables those occasions to be reduced but it is difficult to be in a perfect viewing position every time.

Referees are not allowed to assume anything. For example, a ball is rolling towards your opponents' goal and you are sure you are going to get a goal but a spectator steps into the goalmouth and stops it. The referee cannot award the goal because the ball didn't actually pass into the goal.

When you criticize an assistant referee for an offside signal can you appreciate the three observations he has had to make to come to his decision? Where was the attacker in relation to the defenders? Was he in an offside position when the ball was last played by a colleague? Was he involved in active play? You are often so wrapped up in play that you make the judgement when the ball arrives and a lot can happen to change circumstances in those few seconds. Assistant referees don't flag immediately when they see a player in an offside position. They wait to see if the player becomes actively involved in the play so please don't accuse them of a 'late flag' – they have to wait and see.

By reading this book you will discover a lot you didn't know and hopefully it will increase your enjoyment of the game. Even better, it may make you want to take up refereeing – The FA needs your services!

The Referees' Association (RA) offers referees help, guidance and social contact with other referees. Often people are confused over the organization of referees in England so an explanation might be helpful.

The governing body for football in every country is the National Federation – The Football Association (The FA) in England. The FA is part of a group of countries in Europe that form a Confederation – Union of European Football Associations (UEFA). There are six other Confederations – or regional groupings of countries – throughout the world that together form FIFA. There are currently 204 countries in the world registered with FIFA through the seven Confederations. FIFA allocates a number of positions for international referees and assistant referees to each country. Currently The FA has ten male international referees and one female. It also has ten male international assistant referees and two females.

In England, The FA controls refereeing. For professional football The FA works in partnership with The FA Premier League and The Football League to provide for the needs of referees in the professional game. Seventy-five referees and 223 assistant referees are professional game match officials. Of these, currently 21 referees operate as employees, which means that they can choose to be full-time referees and are on the

Select Group. Forty-six assistant referees who are also on the Select Group support them but they are not employed. The Select Group referees and their assistants operate on FA Premier League matches and a few high profile Football League matches.

Statistic

Below the professional level there are **29,500** referees working to support football at a variety of levels of competition in England.

Referees operating in local grassroots football register with their local County Football Association and are entered on the database maintained by The FA. County Associations are supported by FA Regional Referee Managers and take care of the recruitment, initial training, allocation to leagues, further training and promotion of referees in their areas up to senior county referee status. Referees are ascribed a level between one and ten according to the level of competition in which they officiate. Referees progress through the promotion pyramid following assessment of their performance at each stage.

The FA runs an organization to inform, support and educate all referees, but especially those not involved in the professional game. This is called The FA Match Officials' Association (FAMOA).

The RA is an independent organization that referees can join, in order to gain additional benefits. By joining this Association referees can benefit from guidance and assistance in their promotion ambitions by listening to the advice of more senior colleagues. The RA also runs a very good personal insurance scheme, assists with training, carries a good range of referees' kit and equipment for sale and produces a monthly magazine.

Schools of Excellence, Referee Academies and Refereeing Schools are organized in each area of England in order to provide maximum benefit from training opportunities in both physical and mental preparation. Referees who take these training opportunities are guided towards good habits, given expert training in refereeing techniques, gain experience in a controlled environment and are encouraged to take a positive approach towards maintaining fitness levels.

Chapter 1

Referees and the Laws of the Game

THIS CHAPTER WILL:
- Introduce the 17 Laws of the Game.
- Put each of these Laws into context.

It is essential to begin this book by focusing on the 17 Laws of the Game since it is the knowledge of these Laws that forms the foundations of all refereeing.

The International Football Association Board (IFAB) first agreed the Laws of the Game when it was founded in 1886. Since then there have been few changes made to these Laws, as the IFAB believes that they should be kept as simple and as straightforward as possible.

The IFAB consists of the four British Associations and FIFA. It meets annually and its decisions are binding on all National Associations. No alterations to the Laws of the Game may be made by any Association until the Board has passed them.

The primary aim of the IFAB is consistent Law interpretation and application so as to ensure that the Laws can be applied in the same way at any level of football from the World Cup Final to a friendly game in a local park.

The Laws are few in number and are quite simply stated. Below is an outline of each Law that should provide you with the essential principles on which to base an understanding of refereeing. Some of these Laws may at first seem complicated, however they will be revisited, illustrated and explained in greater detail throughout the book.

Law 1 – The field of play

Referees are expected to conduct pitch inspections to ensure the safety of players. For this they need to know the measurements of the field of play and the size and functions of areas such as the goal and penalty areas.

The required dimensions of the field of play are as follows:

- **Length**: Minimum 100 yards (90 m); maximum 130 yards (120 m).
- **Width**: Minimum 50 yards (45 m); maximum 100 yards (90 m).

The measurements of the field of play (the pitch) can vary but the inner dimensions remain the same (Chapter 2 will look at this in more detail).

Figure 1 **The field of play**

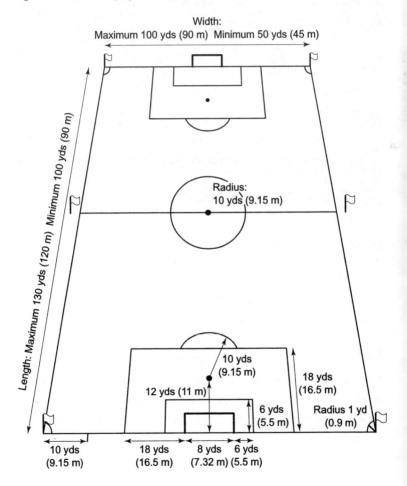

The field of play is marked with lines (not more than 5 in/12 cm wide) which are included as part of the playing area. This has interesting implications for fouls committed on the lines of the penalty area, as if a foul is committed by the defending team on this line, a penalty should be awarded.

The two longer boundary lines are called touchlines and the two shorter lines are called goal lines. The centre mark is indicated at the midpoint of the halfway line. A circle with a radius of 10 yards (9.15 m) is marked around it.

Quote | 'Without goals there would be no purpose to football!'

The referee needs to learn the correct dimensions of the goal and penalty areas. The referee also has to check the nets and know exactly what to do if a crossbar or goalpost breaks (please refer to Chapter 2 page 33). At all times the referee must be aware of goalpost safety; goals must be anchored securely to the ground and portable goals may only be used if the referee can satisfy this requirement.

Dimensions of the goal area

Two lines are drawn at right angles to the goal line, 6 yards (5.5 m) from the inside of each goalpost. These lines extend into the field of play for a distance of 6 yards (5.5 m) and are joined by a line drawn parallel with the goal line.

Dimensions of the penalty area

The referee must know the exact dimensions of the penalty area as the decisions a referee has to make regarding offences committed in the penalty area are often the decisions that will have the greatest influence on the result of a match. If a foul is committed by the defending team in the penalty area (or on the line of the penalty area) the referee will award a penalty kick to the attacking team. The penalty area is most commonly remembered as the limit to the goalkeeper's handling area.

Two lines are drawn at right angles to the goal line, 18 yards (16.5 m) from the inside of each goalpost. These lines extend into the field of play for 18 yards (16.5 m) and are joined by a line drawn parallel with the goal line.

The referee also needs to be conscious of the safety of players when inspecting the corner areas. A flag post, which is too short, or one that has a sharp top, can be dangerous. These flag posts must be placed at the four corners of the pitch and should be no less than 5 feet (1.5 m) high. If halfway line flags are used they must be set back not less than 1 yard (0.9 m) outside the touchline. A quarter circle with a radius of 1 yard (0.9 m) from each corner flag post must be drawn inside the field of play. This is known as the corner arc.

Law 2 – The ball

As with the dimensions of the field of play, there can be variation in the size of the ball for young players, women and veterans. Referees must be familiar with the expected shapes, size, weight and pressure of the ball. It is up to the referee to decide that each ball used meets the requirements of the Law.

The permitted requirements of the ball are as follows:

- Circumference of not more than 28 inches (70 cm), no less than 27 inches (6.8 cm).
- Weight of the ball at the start of the match of no more than 16 oz (450 g), no less than 14 oz (410 g).
- Pressure of the ball equal to 0.6–1.1 atmospheres (600–1,100 g/cm^2) at sea level (8.5 lbs/sq in 15.6 lbs/sq in).

The referee must examine the ball's surface for all possibilities of danger to players. He must know exactly what to do if a ball becomes defective or bursts during the game. The ball may not be changed during the match without the authority of the referee. Balls are expensive and it is the referee's responsibility to see that they are returned to the home club at the end of the game.

Law 3 – The number of players

The game is designed for the enjoyment of players. The Laws try to provide for equality of opportunity for the two teams and therefore there are restrictions concerning the number of players allowed and how many can be replaced by substitutes. Fundamentally, each team must consist of no more than 11 players, one of whom is the goalkeeper – the goalkeeper has a special significance and is referred to in almost every Law. A match may not continue if either team consists of fewer than seven players.

Different regulations apply to matches in leagues or competitions than to friendly matches such as pre-season games or benefit matches. The referee needs to be familiar with the rules governing the different competitions in which he referees. For example, if the game is a friendly match, the opposing managers may come to an agreement to allow 11 substitutes in each team, however in an official competition organized under the authority of FIFA, the Confederations or the National Associations, the rules will only allow for three substitutes to be used (although up to seven may be nominated).

In all matches, whether they are pre-season friendlies or the FA Cup Final, the names of the substitutes must be given to the referee prior to the start of the match. Any substitutes not named before the match will not be able to take part.

Quote | 'Remember, no name, no game!'

The referee must be in control of the game at all times. This means that he must be informed before any proposed substitution is made. The substitute may only take to the field after the player who is being replaced has left the field of play and the referee has signalled for the substitute to assume his position on the pitch.

The role of the referee cannot be underestimated since all substitutes are subject to the authority and jurisdiction of the referee, whether on or off the pitch. If a substitution occurs without the referee's permission (including the substitution of the goalkeeper) play must be stopped, the substitute cautioned, shown the yellow card and asked to leave the pitch before returning using the proper procedure.

You may recall seeing small areas marked around the trainers' benches. These are the technical areas and the referee has to be aware of the restrictions placed upon team officials who wish to pass on instructions to their players.

As with all the Laws the referee has to understand what to do to punish offenders and how and where to restart the game after each incident.

Law 4 – The players' equipment

The referee must not underestimate his responsibility regarding the safety of players. Sometimes players even have to be reminded that they can put themselves in danger – by wearing earrings, for example. Before the start of each game, the referee must take all reasonable steps to ensure the safety of the players. This includes making sure that each player is protected adequately by shinguards and that goalkeepers are easily identifiable (this is why they wear different coloured shirts).

<table>
<tr><td>Quote</td><td>'Ever wondered why goalkeepers sometimes wear bright and outlandish coloured shirts? There is a practical reason for this – to distinguish them from their team-mates.'</td></tr>
</table>

All these checks will not only ensure the safety of everyone involved in the game but will also help avoid confusion over the specific duties and privileges of each player and the responsibilities of the referee (see Chapter 2, page 38).

The referee must make the appropriate decision if any aspects of this Law are infringed. This may mean that the player at fault should be instructed by the referee to leave the field of play and only return (when signalled by the referee) once they have the correct equipment. A player who has been required to leave the field of play because of an infringement of this Law and who enters (or re-enters) the field of play without the referee's permission should be cautioned and shown the yellow card. The player in question can only leave the field of play when the ball ceases to be in play and likewise can only re-enter the field of play when the ball is out of play.

Law 5 – The referee

Refereeing can be an enjoyable experience but it is also a responsible job with demanding duties. Most significantly, it is the referee's job to enforce the Laws of the Game. Below is a list of the main powers and duties of the referee (these will be looked at in greater detail in Chapter 4).

- Controls the match in co-operation with the assistant referees and, where applicable, with the fourth official.
- Acts as timekeeper and keeps a record of the match.
- Stops, suspends or terminates the match, at his discretion, for any infringements of the Laws.

- Stops, suspends or terminates the match because of outside interference of any kind.

- Stops the match if, in his opinion, a player is seriously injured and ensures that they are removed from the field of play.

- Allows play to continue until the ball is out of play if a player is, in his opinion, only slightly injured.

- Ensures that any player bleeding from a wound leaves the field of play. The player may only return on receiving a signal from the referee, who must be satisfied that the bleeding has stopped.

- Allows play to continue when the team against which an offence has been committed will benefit from such an advantage and penalizes the original offence if the anticipated advantage does not ensue at that time.

- Punishes the more serious offence when a player commits more than one offence at the same time.

- Takes disciplinary action against players guilty of cautionable and sending-off offences. He is not obliged to take this action immediately but must do so when the ball next goes out of play.

- Takes action against team officials who fail to conduct themselves in a responsible manner and may at his discretion, expel them from the field of play and its immediate surrounds.

- Acts on the advice of assistant referees regarding incidents which he has not seen.

- Ensures that no unauthorized persons enter the field of play.

- Restarts the match after it has been stopped.

- Provides the appropriate authorities with a match report which includes information on any disciplinary action taken against players, and/or team officials and any other incidents which occurred before, during or after the match.

Referees don't have the benefit of slow-motion replays to review their decisions but if a mistake has been made the referee can change the decision, as long as play has not restarted. He can also get advice from the assistant referee in this respect. The referee may decide that although an offence has been committed it would be worth allowing play to continue if the side offended against could gain an advantage. Remember, if the team doesn't gain the anticipated advantage immediately, the referee can still award the original free kick. The most important thing to note is that the referee's decision is final.

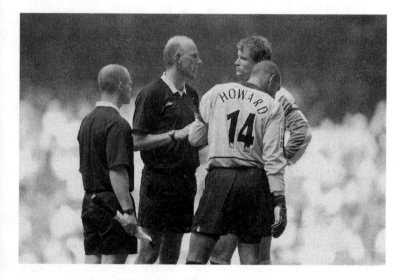

Law 6 – The assistant referees

Referees will often be helped by people running the line (assistant referees). In the referee's early matches it is quite likely that these assistants will be club officials, or even substitutes waiting for their turn to play.

Assistants have specific duties, according to their qualifications and experience and it is important to remember that assistant referees never make a decision. They signal to the referee to indicate they want to draw his attention to something they may be in a better position to see. However, the final decision is the referee's whether the assistant is a club official or a neutral assistant.

The main duties of an assistant referee are to indicate to the referee the circumstances below (Chapter 5 will study these in more detail):

- When the whole of the ball has passed out of the field of play.
- Which side is entitled to a corner kick, goal kick or throw-in.
- When a player may be penalized for being in an offside position.
- When a substitution is requested.
- When misconduct or any other incident has occurred out of the view of the referee.
- When offences have been committed whenever the assistants are closer to the action than the referee (this includes, in particular circumstances, offences committed in the penalty area).
- Whether, at penalty kicks, the goalkeeper has moved forward before the ball has been kicked and if the ball has crossed the line.

Law 7 – The duration of the match

A match normally consists of two equal periods of 45 minutes with an interval of up to 15 minutes. Competition rules may allow some modification of these arrangements but any agreement to alter the periods of play must be made before the start of the match and must comply with competition rules. Players are entitled to an interval at half-time.

Commentators often speak of time added on at the end of each half. This is because the referee will need to allow for time lost through a number of events, including assessment of injury to players, removal of injured players from the field of play for treatment, substitutions and wasting time. In some competitions extra time is allowed to produce a result, thereby avoiding the need for a replay.

It must be remembered that the allowance for any time lost is always at the discretion of the referee.

Law 8 – The start and restart of play

The referee should try to make a good impression at the start of play. Self-confidence impresses the two teams and lets them feel that they are privileged to have such a confident and self-assured referee.

Before the game can start, a coin must be tossed. The team that wins the toss decides which goal it will attack in the first half of the match and takes the kick-off to start the second half of the match; the team that loses takes the kick-off at the beginning of the game. It must be remembered that at half-time the teams change ends and attack opposite goals.

After such preliminaries, the game 'kicks off'. This is a way of starting or re-starting play either at the start of the match, after a goal has been scored, at the start of the second half or at the start of each period of extra time.

Many kick-offs are incorrectly taken with at least one player in their opponents' half ready to play the ball back to their defender. This is not permitted. Referees should correct this and make a good impression right from the start of the game.

Another important point to note is that the kicker who takes the kick-off must not touch the ball a second time until it has touched another player. At all times and in all situations in which a kick-off can take place, the referee must be in complete control. A kick-off can only happen if the referee has signalled for it.

If this law is infringed the kick-off is retaken, except if the kicker touches the ball a second time before it has touched another player; in this case, the referee must award an indirect free kick to the opposing team.

When the referee has had to stop the game without an infringement being committed, for example if the ball becomes unplayable, he will drop the ball. The Law describes the correct procedure, although in practice, in order to see fair play, agreement between the teams often allows for one team to return the ball to the team that was disadvantaged by the stoppage.

The correct procedure for a dropped ball is as follows: the referee should drop the ball at the place where it was located when the play was stopped. Play restarts when the ball touches the ground.

Law 9 – Ball in and out of play

One of the principal roles of the referee is to indicate when the ball is in or out of play. This is important because offences committed whilst the ball is out of play are punished differently.

According to the Law, the ball is out of play when 'it has wholly crossed the goal line or touch line whether on the ground or in the air' or when 'play has been stopped by the referee'.

The ball remains in play when it rebounds from a goalpost, crossbar or corner flag post and remains in the field of play or when it rebounds from either the referee or an assistant referee when he is on the field of play.

Figure 2 **In or out of play**

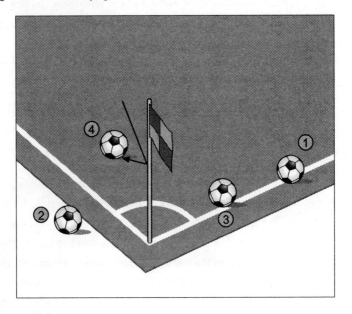

① **Ball in play**
② **Ball out of play**
③ **Ball in play**
④ **Ball rebounding from corner flagpost, goalpost or crossbar into field is in play.**

Law 10 – The method of scoring

Although it may seem obvious to anyone with the faintest knowledge of football, it is nevertheless important to know what 'officially' constitutes a goal scored. According to the Laws of the Game, a goal is scored when 'the whole of the ball passes over the goal line, between the goalposts and under the crossbar' (this is dependent upon there having been no

Figure 3 **A goal scored**

infringement of the Laws prior to scoring the goal). The whole purpose of Association Football is to score goals. This is how a game is decided. If the game is a draw at the end of the match some competitions have rules to ensure that a decision is reached through extra time or by kicks from the penalty mark.

Law 11 – Offside

Knowing this Law is often used to measure people's football knowledge. If you can explain this one then you're well on the way to becoming an expert!

According to the Law, a player is offside when 'he is nearer to his opponents' goal line than both the ball and the second last opponent'. On the other hand, a player is *not* offside if he is 'in his own half of the field of play' or 'he is level with the second last opponent' or he 'is level with the last two opponents'. (Chapter 6 concentrates solely on the offside Law.)

It must be remembered that it is not an offence in itself to be in an offside position and a player should not be penalized if the ball is received directly from a goal kick, a throw-in or a corner kick. However, it becomes an offence if, at the moment the ball touches or is played by one of his team, the player is, in the opinion of the referee, involved in active play by 'interfering with an opponent', or 'interfering with play' or 'gaining an advantage by being in that position'.

The penalty for an offside offence is easy to remember: the referee awards an indirect free kick to the opposing team, to be taken from the place where the infringement occurred.

Best Practice Referees should ask themselves:

- Is the player in an offside position?
- Are there any circumstances that prevent them from being given offside?
- What were the circumstances when a colleague last played the ball?
- Are they involved in active play?
- How do I restart play?

Law 12 – Fouls and misconduct

A referee's job is to ensure that each team can play the game safely and fairly. It is for this reason that the referee must be on the lookout for fouls or instances of misconduct and penalize them accordingly.

Below is a list of the **cautionable (yellow card) offences**:

- Unsporting behaviour.
- Showing dissent by word or action.
- Persistent infringement of the Laws of the Game.
- Delaying the restart of play.

- Failing to respect the required distance when play is restarted with a corner kick or free kick.
- Entering or re-entering the field of play without the referee's permission.
- Deliberately leaving the field of play without the referee's permission.

The following list details the **sending-off (red card) offences**:

- Serious foul play.
- Violent conduct.
- Spitting at an opponent or any other person.
- Denying the opposing team a goal or an obvious goal-scoring opportunity by deliberately handling the ball (this does not apply to a goalkeeper within his own penalty area).
- Denying an obvious goal-scoring opportunity to an opponent moving towards the player's goal by an offence punishable by a free kick or a penalty kick.
- Offensive, insulting or abusive language and/or gestures.
- Receiving a second caution in the same match.

Other than showing the yellow and red cards there are other, often crucial, sanctions that must be awarded to the opposition in the instance of misconduct. These are the direct free kick, the penalty kick and the indirect free kick. The ten offences that are punished by direct free kicks or penalty kicks are as follows:

- Kicking or attempting to kick an opponent.
- Tripping or attempting to trip an opponent.
- Jumping at an opponent.
- Charging at an opponent.
- Striking or attempting to strike an opponent.
- Pushing an opponent.

A direct free kick is also awarded to the opposing team if a player:

- **Tackles an opponent to gain possession of the ball, making contact with the opponent before touching the ball.**
- **Holds an opponent.**
- **Spits at an opponent.**
- **Handles the ball deliberately (except for the goalkeeper within his own penalty area).**

A penalty kick is awarded if any of the above ten offences are committed by a player inside his own penalty area, irrespective of the position of the ball, provided it is in play.

An indirect free kick is awarded to the opposing team if a goalkeeper, inside his own penalty area, commits any of the following four offences:

- **Takes more than six seconds while controlling the ball with his hands before releasing it from his possession.**
- **Touches the ball again with his hands after it has been released from his possession and has not touched any other player.**
- **Touches the ball with his hands after it has been deliberately kicked to him by a team-mate.**
- **Touches the ball with his hands after he has received it directly from a throw-in taken by a team-mate.**

An indirect free kick is also awarded to the opposing team if a player, in the opinion of the referee:

- **Plays in a dangerous manner.**
- **Impedes the progress of an opponent.**
- **Prevents the goalkeeper from releasing the ball from his hands.**
- **Commits any other offence, not previously mentioned in Law 12, for which play is stopped to caution or dismiss a player.**

Chapter 7 expands on this Law, and provides greater detail on the types of fouls, misconduct and awards that should be given.

In managing players it is important to decide where to start on the staircase of punishments. It is up to the referee to decide on the seriousness of the offence and the attitude of the player to discipline. On some occasions the strong whistle, a quiet word of warning or a more public rebuke will be sufficient. On other occasions the referee will be aware that anything short of a caution will be inappropriate or seen as a sign of weakness.

Law 13 – Free kicks

There are two types of free kick: indirect or direct. For both of these the ball must be stationary when the kick is taken and the kicker must not touch the ball a second time until it has touched another player. When a direct free kick is awarded to a team the kicker can score direct from the kick into his opponents' goal. For less serious offences indirect free kicks are awarded. A goal cannot be scored direct; another player must touch or play the ball first.

If a direct free kick is kicked into the opponents' goal, a goal is awarded.

The referee indicates an indirect free kick by raising his arm above his head. He should maintain his arm in this position until the kick has been taken and the ball has touched another player or has gone out of play. A goal can only be scored if the ball subsequently touches another player before it enters the goal. If an indirect free kick is kicked directly into the opponents' goal, a goal kick is awarded.

The position of any free kick, direct or indirect, is very important. In the case of a direct or indirect free kick to the defending team in their own penalty area, all opponents must be at least 10 yards (9.15 m) from the ball and must remain outside the penalty area until the ball is in play (when the ball is kicked directly beyond the penalty area). Any free kick awarded in the defenders' goal area is taken from any point inside that area.

In the case of an indirect free kick to the attacking team, all opponents must be at least 10 yards (9.15 m) from the ball until it is in play (when it is kicked), unless they are on their own goal line between the goalposts. An indirect free kick awarded to the attacking team inside the defenders' goal area is taken from that part of the goal area line which runs parallel to the goal line, at the point nearest to where the infringement occurred.

Figure 4 **Goal area**

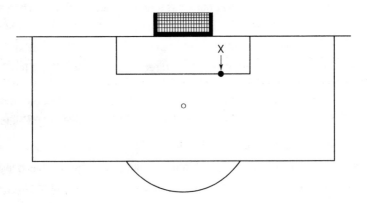

X = where offence occurred
● = where free kick is taken

In the case of a free kick outside the penalty area, all opponents must be at least 10 yards (9.15 m) from the ball until it is in play (when it is kicked and moves).

The referee has to decide what type of offence has been committed, and from this whether it is to be penalized with a direct or an indirect free kick. A direct free kick is upgraded to a penalty kick if it is committed by a defender in his own penalty area.

It is also important to remember that neither a direct nor an indirect free kick can result in a goal if it goes directly into the kicker's own goal – the goal can only be scored against the offending team.

Law 14 – The penalty kick

A penalty kick is awarded against a team that commits one of the ten offences for which a direct free kick is awarded inside its own penalty area. The ball has to be in play at the time of the offence. Penalty kicks usually result in goals so they are incredibly important decisions, especially when additional time has to be allowed for them to be taken at the end of either half-time or at the end of extra time.

As with all facets of the game, the referee must be in control at all times. Therefore, after awarding the kick the referee's next responsibility is to see that the kick is taken properly. He must ensure that the ball is placed on the penalty mark and the player who is going to take the kick has been properly identified ie: the goalkeeper and the referee need to know who is taking the kick. The defending goalkeeper must be on his goal line facing the kicker until the ball has been kicked.

All other players must be on the field of play, outside the penalty area and at least 10 yards (9.15 m) from the ball and behind the ball. The arc drawn outside the penalty area helps the referee to check the position of the players. The referee should only signal for the kick when all these conditions are correctly complied with.

As with all Laws there are sanctions for non-compliance. If the player taking the kick offends, the referee will wait to see the result of the kick and insist it is taken again if he scores. If he plays the ball a second time before another player touches it, an indirect free kick is awarded against the kicker. Referees have to watch for the ball rebounding from the crossbar or goalposts to the kicker because, as no other player has touched it, he cannot play it again.

Figure 5 **Penalty**

If the goalkeeper moves forward off their line before the ball is kicked the referee waits to see if a goal is scored. If it is scored then the goal stands. If the kick is saved or misses the goal the kicker gets another chance.

If players enter the penalty area before the kick is taken the referee again awaits the result of the kick. If it is the defending team and a goal is scored he allows the goal. If the kick is saved or misses the goal the referee awards a retake of the kick.

If attacking players enter the area before the kick is taken the reverse happens. If the kick results in a goal it is retaken but if it is saved or misses, the kicker does not get a second chance.

If players of both teams go into the area before the kick is taken the penalty kick has to be taken again.

All of this sounds very complicated but the simple rule of thumb is to remember that any player breaking the Law cannot be seen to gain an advantage from offending.

Law 15 – The throw-in

A throw-in is a method of restarting play when the ball has gone out of play over the touchlines. The throw-in is awarded to the opponents of the player who last touched the ball.

The correct procedure is as follows: the player who is throwing in must face the field of play and have part of each foot either on the touchline or on the ground outside the touchline. Both hands must be used as he delivers the ball from behind and over his head. Most importantly, the thrower may not touch the ball again until it has touched another player. The ball must be thrown from the 'point' at which it passed over the line and the ball is in play when it enters the field of play.

As with all of the Laws there are always going to be infringements of this procedure that will demand sanctions imposed by the referee.

In the case of the thrower touching the ball a second time (except with his hands) before it has touched another player, the referee must award an indirect free kick to the opposing team. If, after the ball is in play, the thrower deliberately handles the ball before it has touched another player, a direct free kick must be awarded to the opposing team; a penalty kick is awarded if the infringement occurs inside the thrower's penalty area.

When the goalkeeper takes the throw-in different rules and sanctions apply. If, after the ball is in play, the goalkeeper touches the ball a second time (except with his hands) before it has touched another player, the referee must award an indirect free kick to the opposing team. If, after the ball is in play, the goalkeeper deliberately handles the ball before it

Figure 6 **Throw-in procedure**

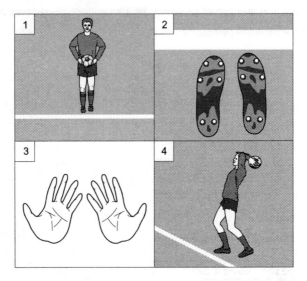

At the moment of delivering the ball, the thrower: ① faces the field of play ② has part of each foot either on the touch line or on the ground outside the touch line ③ uses both hands ④ delivers the ball from behind and over his head.

has touched another player a direct free kick is awarded to the opposing team. If the infringement occurred inside the goalkeeper's penalty area, an indirect free kick is awarded.

If any opponent unfairly distracts or impedes the thrower, the referee must caution them for unsporting behaviour and show them the yellow card.

Further to all of the above, there are three more important aspects to remember:

- A goal cannot be scored directly from a throw-in.
- If the throw-in is not taken correctly the throw is awarded to the other team.
- A goalkeeper cannot receive the ball directly into his hands when a colleague takes a throw-in.

Law 16 – The goal kick

A goal kick is a method of restarting play after the ball has crossed the goal line outside the goals when a member of the attacking team has last touched it.

A player of the defending team then kicks the ball from any point within the goal area whilst the opponents remain outside the penalty area until the ball is in play. The kicker must not play the ball a second time until another player has touched it.

If the ball is not kicked directly into play beyond the penalty area the kick is retaken. If, after the ball is in play, the kicker touches the ball a second time (except with his hands) before it has touched another player, an indirect free kick is awarded to the opposing team. If, after the ball is in play, the kicker deliberately handles the ball before it has touched another player, the referee must award a direct free kick to the opposing team. A penalty kick should be awarded if the infringement occurred inside the kicker's penalty area. This would only happen on rare occasions as the ball would need to have left the penalty area to be in play and be blown back in again.

As with other Laws, there are slightly different sanctions for the goalkeeper. If, when the goalkeeper takes the goal kick, he touches the ball a second time after it has passed into play, the referee should award an indirect free kick to the opposing team. If, after the ball is in play, the goalkeeper deliberately handles the ball before it has touched another player, a direct free kick is awarded to the opposing team. If the infringement has occurred outside the goalkeeper's penalty area, the kick should be taken from the place where the infringement occurred.

For any other infringement of this Law the kick should be retaken.

The referee must ensure that the ball and the players are correctly positioned before giving the signal for the goal kick. The best position for the referee is level with where the ball will land and looking into play.

Law 17 – The corner kick

A corner kick is a method of restarting play after the ball has crossed the goal line outside the goals, when a member of the defending team has last touched it.

After awarding a corner kick the referee should ensure that the ball is placed inside the corner arc at the nearest corner flag post; the flag post must not be removed. Opponents should remain at least 10 yards (9.15 m) from the ball until it is in play. A player of the attacking team must kick the ball and this kicker must not play the ball a second time until it has touched another player.

If, after the ball is in play, the kicker touches the ball a second time (except with his hands) before it has touched another player, the referee should award an indirect free kick to the opposing team. If, after the ball is in play, the kicker deliberately handles the ball before it has touched another player, the referee should award a direct free kick to the opposing team.

For any other infringements the kick is to be retaken.

The referee needs to be in a good position to see that the ball and the players are correctly positioned and he needs to have a good clear view of the players who are contesting the ball as it comes down to ground level. He must watch the players *not* the ball and try to find a position where the players do not block his view.

The referee should stay around the penalty area until he is convinced there is no longer a possibility of a goal-line decision or an offside position.

Summary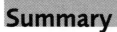

- A good knowledge of the Laws of the Game is indispensable to anyone involved in football.

- The referee must be in control at all times.

- It is up to the referee to ensure that the game is played safely and fairly.

Self testers

1 Name three of the main duties of the referee.
2 How long should a game usually last?
3 How many players is a team allowed?

Action plan

Write down all the questions that you may have as a result of reading this chapter and use this for reference whilst reading the remainder of the book to ensure you gain a full understanding.

LEARNING

Chapter 2

Before a game can start

THIS CHAPTER WILL:
- Explain how the Laws develop and evolve.
- Look at the key aspects for a referee before the game starts.
- Review the checks that must be made on the equipment used before the game starts.

The Laws are few in number (17) and are quite simply stated. Some differences in the interpretation of the Laws of the Game have developed over the years.

The IFAB is of the opinion that the Laws should be kept as simple and straightforward as possible. Differences of application should be resolved by 'rulings or decisions' rather than by further amendments to the Laws. FIFA produces a book of questions and answers to communicate these decisions.

In order to maintain consistent application of Law the responsibility for giving interpretations over specific happenings is left to the International

FA Board. In this context, FIFA *alone* has the specific duty to communicate all relevant amendments and/or decisions to the National Associations affiliated to FIFA.

Consistent Law interpretation and application must be achieved. Not all aspects of the Laws are fully understood, especially when unusual things happen.

▨   Before we explain all the key elements that must be taken into account before a game starts, what do you think these key elements will be?

Law 1 deals with the field of play

Referees have a duty of care to all participants. This leads them to make pitch inspections to ensure that elements of danger are eliminated. Bad weather or poor maintenance of the ground puts safe participation in doubt. Pitch markings and corner flags need to be checked to see that all is in order. If the corner flag posts are too short or have a pointed top they could be dangerous to players coming into contact with them at speed.

Figure 7

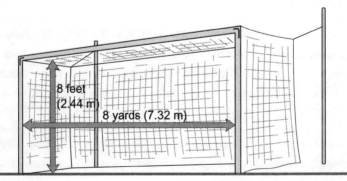

There is no point having nets if they 'leak'. They must be pegged down and secured to the posts and crossbar if they are to do their job efficiently.

Quote | 'Although nets have holes, make sure they are not too big!'

There is a good deal of flexibility in the outer dimensions of the field of play. This is to enable football to be played wherever there is a reasonably sized playing area. Where there is more space available, the football produced is often of a higher quality with room for players to show their skills. Whatever the size of the pitch, the inner markings – the penalty and goal areas etc. – are of a standard size.

The length of the field of play can be as much as 130 yards (120 m) or as little as 100 yards (90 m). The width can vary from a maximum of 100 yards (90 m) to a minimum of 50 yards (45 m).

Studying these figures you might think that the pitch could be square but this is not the case. The field of play must be rectangular. The length of the touchlines must be greater than the length of the goal lines.

Rules of various competitions will often stipulate the size of the playing area within the limits set by the Laws of the Game. For example in international matches the maximum length is 120 yards (110 m) and the minimum is 110 yards (100 m). The width in international matches must be no more than 82 yards (75 m) and no less than 70 yards (64 m).

Field markings

The boundaries of the field of play have to be clearly marked to show when the ball is in or out of play. The lines are part of the playing area so the ball must wholly cross these lines to be out of play. The lines marking out the areas within the field of play are also part of the area they mark out.

Lines marking out all areas should be distinct and should not be more than 5 inches (12 cm) wide.

Quote | 'Clear pitch markings are essential to assist a number of the referee's decisions.'

There are two purposes for the centre line. Firstly, it helps the referee to see that each player is in his own half at the kick-off. The referee is further helped by a circle of 10 yards (9.15 m) radius to indicate how close the opponents can be at the kick-off.

The second function concerns offside. A player can not be in an offside position if he is in his own half of the field of play. Chapter 6 gives further information about offside.

The corner arc
The player taking a corner is allowed to position the ball anywhere inside the quarter circle, including the line marking it out.

It is quite common now to find a mark off the field of play, 10 yards (9.15 m) from the corner arc along the goal lines to help officials check that opposing players are the correct distance from the corner kick.

Flag posts
There may also be flag posts at each end of the halfway line, but they must be at least 1 yard (0.9 m) outside the touchline so that they do not get in the way of play.

Goals
It is important that both goalposts and the crossbar have the same width and depth, which do not exceed 5 inches (12 cm). The dimensions of the posts, crossbar and line must match so that the referee can judge that a goal has been scored, by the ball completely passing into goal. The goalposts and crossbars must be white.

Goalposts and crossbars must be made of wood, metal or other approved material. Their shape may be square, rectangular, round or elliptical and they must not be dangerous to players.

If the crossbar falls down or breaks, the referee must stop play until it has been repaired or replaced. If a repair is not possible the referee has no choice but to abandon the match. A rope cannot be used to replace the crossbar, as the ball will not rebound from it properly. If the broken post or crossbar can be repaired, the referee will restart the match with a dropped ball at the place where the ball was when play was stopped. If this was in the goal area the referee would take the ball to the nearest point on the goal area line and drop it on the edge of the goal area.

Goalpost safety

Goalkeepers have been injured by temporary goalposts that topple over. Goals must be anchored securely to the ground. Portable goals may only be used if they satisfy this requirement.

The FA has promoted the importance of goalpost safety for a number of years as players have died in the past from accidents involving poorly maintained goalposts.

■ Find out more about The FA's goalpost safety campaign by visiting **www.TheFA.com**.

Law 2 deals with the ball

Quote | 'The most essential piece of equipment is always the ball!'

We couldn't have a game of football without a ball and Law 2 deals with specifications and other details. FIFA has been even more specific over the criteria for manufacturers to follow and insists that balls carry logos that ensure these requirements have been met for its competitions. Referees in non-FIFA competitions accept any ball that satisfies the normal requirements of Law 2.

Replacement of a defective ball

It is unusual for the ball to burst but it may become soft during the game. If the referee stops the match it will be restarted with a dropped ball. If it happens whilst the ball is out of play the game will start with the usual restart.

Best Practice All clubs must make sure that they have enough footballs available in case they become defective or are lost (for example, kicked into a tree or a neighbouring garden) as without a ball you won't be able to finish the game!

Permission to change the ball

At professional games we often see ball boys or girls carrying spare balls to throw on to keep the game flowing. This is known as the 'multi-ball' system. We don't want anyone throwing on a replacement ball when players least expect it, therefore, technically the ball may not be changed during the match without the permission of the referee. In other words, the referee should indicate when he wants the ball replaced and double check that it meets the requirements of the Law. When the multi-ball system is in use the referee checks all possible balls before the game.

Law 3 deals with the players

A match may not start if either team has less than seven players. The advice of the International Board is that a match should not continue if there are fewer than seven players in either team.

Recently, history was made in a Football League match where the game was abandoned because one team was reduced to less than seven players by injury and dismissals. Had the game continued it would have been reduced to a farce.

Substitutes

We are now familiar with the use of substitutes to replace injured players or for tactical reasons. Regulations vary according to competition rules and are more relaxed in friendly games that are arranged to allow more players to participate over the period of the game.

In friendly matches when there is nothing at stake in the game more substitutes are allowed. In these games a maximum of six substitutes can be used.

Statistic

Substitutes were first used in **1965**.

The substitution is completed when a substitute enters the field of play and from that moment, the substitute becomes a player. The replaced player ceases to be a player and can take no further part in the match.

The referee has to be in charge of all that is going on and so has authority over substitutes and players. This is true whether the substitutes have been called on to play or not. In other words, they are still under the referee's control and can be disciplined whether they are playing, warming up or still on the trainers' bench.

Quote | 'Referees control all the players and team staff, whether they are on the pitch or the sidelines.'

If a substitute enters the field of play without the referee's permission, play is stopped, the substitute is cautioned and has to leave the field of play – he can then join the team using the correct procedure.

Players and substitutes warm up on the pitch and occasionally may do something that causes them to be sent off before the game begins. They may have an old score to settle with an opponent from a previous game. In these circumstances a player sent off under Law 12 before play begins may be replaced only by a named substitute. A team may, therefore, start a match with 11 players even when a player has been ordered off before the kick-off. A further substitute cannot be nominated. A substitute sent off before or during the game may not be replaced.

▨ If you're a coach or involved with a team, make sure that all of your players, coaches and others involved with the team are aware that the referee can still caution or send them off before they even enter the field of play and before the game begins.

Clubs should inform referees of the names of substitutes before a match. A referee usually asks for the names if the secretary forgets to tell him, but strictly speaking 'no name – no game'.

Substitutes may be nominated for two matches taking place at the same time. This sometimes happens on park pitches.

Team officials in the technical area
The coach or any other team official can give tactical instructions to the players during the match – but only one coach or team official can give instructions at a time. They have to stay in the technical area, if there is one, and behave in a responsible manner.

▨ The next time you watch a match where technical areas are used, observe the coaches in this area and see if they are abiding by the rules.

Goalkeepers

The goalkeeper has a specific role and certain privileges. Spectators always consider that the opponents' goalkeeper has the privilege of over-protection by the referee. However, they scream and shout if anyone goes near their keeper. That's their privilege for paying to watch the game.

Quote | 'It is not the role of the referee to protect the goalkeeper.'

Law 4 deals with players' equipment

Safety

As we discussed earlier, a referee has a responsibility to preserve safe playing conditions. This leads him to check that players do not wear anything that may create a dangerous situation for other players or for themselves. Referees should set a good example by removing or taping their own rings and jewellery. Referees, however, should make allowances for religious symbols (e.g. a player of the Sikh religion wearing a Kara in a match), provided that they are not dangerous and that adequate covering is applied as protection.

The referee needs to check carefully to see if rings, earrings, necklaces, plaster casts, footwear or any form of ornamentation on the players' clothing (such as zips) are a possible source of danger.

Spectacles also have to be considered carefully from the safety point of view. Safety sports spectacles are usually fine and don't constitute a danger. They are, however, expensive and referees are often asked to approve ordinary spectacles. Referees have been instructed not to put obstacles in the way of people wanting to play football. If the spectacles a player wears have plastic lenses and safe frames, The FA would want them to be allowed to play.

If the referee notices unsafe equipment during a game, the player will have to leave the field to adjust the equipment. The referee checks again that all is safe before the player joins in again.

Shinguards

It is compulsory for players to wear shinguards. In addition the referee must check that they:

- **Are covered entirely by the stockings.**
- **Are made of a suitable material (rubber, plastic, or similar substance).**
- **Provide a reasonable degree of protection.**

Best Practice Everyone involved in the game needs to realize the importance of players wearing shinguards. Whilst compulsory shinguards are part of the Laws governing football not all players take heed. Everyone involved (referees, coaches and players) need to make sure that players wear them to reduce the potential for injury.

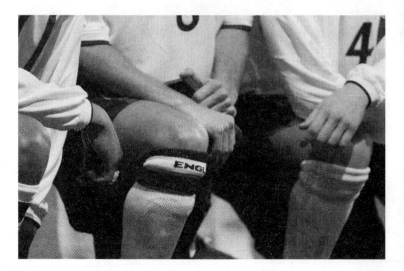

Undershorts

Referees sometimes notice players wearing shorts that show below their team shorts. Usually this is where a strain has occurred and the player is looking after the injury. Law 4 allows this but they must be the same main colour as the team shorts and must not extend beyond the top of the knee.

Shirts

Players' shirts must have sleeves and a player must not reveal an undershirt that contains provocative slogans or advertising.

Summary

- **The playing environment must be thoroughly checked before play can commence.**

- **The size of the field of play can vary but it must be rectangular.**

- **Goalpost safety is a crucial role for the referee.**

- **The referee is in charge of all players and officials whether they are on the pitch, coaching staff or substitutes.**

- **All players must wear shinguards.**

Self testers

1 What is the maximum length a pitch can be?

2 What colour must goalposts be?

3 How many substitutes are allowed in friendly matches?

Action plan

Use this chapter as a guide so that you know what checks are required before a game. Before your next match make sure that all aspects have been completed so that there will be no delays before kick-off.

Chapter 3

LEARNING

Stops, starts and restarts

THIS CHAPTER WILL:
- Help you to understand the different ways of restarting the game after stoppages.
- Explain the correct procedure for penalty shoot outs.
- List the reasons for additional time at the end of each half.

The game starts and stops frequently. The referee has to know the reasons for these interruptions and must respond in an appropriate manner.

Kick-off

The team that wins the toss decides which goal it will attack in the first half. The other team takes the kick-off to start the match. In the second half of the match the teams change ends and attack the opposite goals.

Quote | 'It is very unusual for a goal to be scored directly from the kick-off but the Laws allow this to happen.'

Statistic

The first goalkeeper to score directly from his hands was Pat Jennings playing for Spurs against Manchester United in The FA Charity Shield in **1967**.

Dropped ball

You may have observed the referee starting the game with a dropped ball. It is used if the game has been interrupted with a temporary stoppage, for example, a head injury to a player where the referee decides that to wait for a natural stoppage would be dangerous.

The referee must drop the ball where play was stopped. However, if this were in the goal area he would take it to the goal area line parallel to the goal line otherwise it would be unfair to the defenders.

The ball must touch the ground before it is in play.

Players usually show consideration for each other when a player is injured. If the team kicks the ball out for a colleague to receive attention the other team usually throws the ball back to that team when the game restarts.

▥ The next time you're at a game and the referee stops play, look to see if the game is restarted by a dropped ball.

Restarts in goal areas

We've already mentioned a dropped ball in the goal area. The position of the ball for indirect free kicks to the attacking team in its opponents' goal area is on the goal area line parallel to the goal line nearest to the foul.

Just like a goal kick, a free kick awarded to the defending team inside its own goal area is taken from any point within the goal area.

Free kicks

Most goals nowadays are linked to restarts of play after stoppages. At the taking of free kicks players of the defending team can stand anywhere as long as they are at least 10 yards (9.15 m) from the ball. However, this could be difficult if the free kick is nearer than 10 yards (9.15 m) from the goal. In this case, the players must stand on their own goal line between the goalposts.

The next time an indirect free kick is awarded in the penalty area to the attacking team, in all the mayhem that inevitably happens watch the actions of the referee to see how the situation is controlled.

For free kicks to the defending side in the penalty area the opponents must stay outside the area and at least 10 yards (9.15 m) from the ball and the ball is not in play until it has passed out of the penalty area.

The ball is in play when it is kicked and moves. It is, therefore, permissible for a player to 'flick' the ball up with one or both feet to restart the play. However, the player taking the kick may not touch or play the ball a second time until it has touched or been played by another player.

When play is stopped, the team awarded the free kick sometimes wants to get the ball back into play as quickly as possible – a quick free kick. If an opponent deliberately delays the kick or doesn't go back the correct distance he should be cautioned.

Remember that a team cannot score an 'own goal' with a free kick – direct or indirect. If the ball enters their own goal a corner kick would be awarded.

Figure 8 **The referee makes a clear signal to indicate an indirect free kick**

An indirect free kick must touch or be played by another player (of either team) before passing into goal. If this does not happen a goal kick is the correct restart if the attacking team took the kick.

Penalty kicks

Free kicks near to goal are exciting and fill the spectators of the attacking team with expectation and their opponents with nerves. These feelings are increased tenfold at the award of a penalty kick.

All players except the kicker and the opposing goalkeeper must be on the field of play, outside the penalty area and the penalty arc. They must be behind the penalty mark and cannot come into the area until the kick is taken.

The goalkeeper can move sideways on his line but not forwards until the kick is taken.

Assistant referees watch to see if the goalkeeper advances from his goal line before the kick is taken and whether the ball has crossed the goal line.

A player taking a penalty kick may try to deceive the goalkeeper by 'feinting' – slowing down during the run. This is allowed but he mustn't stop in his run to make the goalkeeper dive early. The player stopping in his run should be cautioned for unsporting behaviour and the kick retaken if a goal is scored.

If half-time or full-time occurs before the penalty kick has been taken, time must be extended to allow it to be taken, or retaken. The referee will wait for a clear result before blowing for time. If the ball enters the goal the result of the kick is obvious. This might be when the ball touches one of the two goalposts, or the crossbar, or goalkeeper, or a combination of these. Providing no infringement has been committed a goal would be allowed.

Retake the penalty or let the goal stand?

If things go wrong at a penalty kick the referee decides if anyone has gained an advantage unfairly. If the player(s) who offended were part of the team gaining the advantage the referee would have the kick retaken.

Examples

- If a goal is scored and the player(s) who offended were in the defending team – goal stands.
- If a goal is missed and the player(s) who offended were in the defending team – retake.
- If a goal is scored and the player(s) who offended were in the team taking the kick – retake.
- If a goal is missed and the player(s) who offended were in the team taking the kick – play continues or goal kick.
- If players of both teams offend – retake.
- If the ball rebounds from the crossbar or the goalpost and is played again by the penalty taker the referee stops play and restarts the match with an indirect free kick to the defending team.
- If attackers encroach and the ball rebounds into play from the crossbar, goalpost or goalkeeper the referee stops play and restarts the match with an indirect free kick to the defending team.

What happens if an outside agent stops the ball?

Anyone – human or animal – not taking part in the game is not allowed to come on to the field of play without the permission of the referee. If an 'outside agent' interferes with a penalty kick by touching the ball, the kick must be retaken.

In other situations, if the game is stopped because of an outside agent the game is restarted with a dropped ball.

Throw-in

A goal cannot be scored directly from a throw-in. If a throw-in taken by the attacking team went directly into goal, play would be restarted by a goal kick. If one taken by the defending team went directly into its own goal, play would be restarted by a corner kick.

Spectators sometimes call for a foul throw if part of the player's foot is past the line. The Law allows part of the foot to be over as long as the thrower has part of each foot either on the touchline or on the ground outside the touchline. Inexperienced players often lift one foot in an effort to throw the ball further – this is a foul throw.

The thrower may not touch the ball again until it has touched another player.

The ball is in play immediately it enters the field of play.

Quote | 'Don't lift your foot from the ground when taking a throw-in.'

Players sometimes stand too close or dance about in front to delay the throw-in or make it difficult for the thrower. The thrower can step back up to 1 yard (0.9 m) to avoid this. If the non-thrower persists and the referee considers it to be unsporting behaviour he will caution the player. The throw-in will then be taken.

There are not many complications to explain for throw-ins. A natural throwing movement starting from behind and over the head will usually result in the ball leaving the hands when they are in front of the vertical plane of the body. This is permitted as long as the throwing movement is continuous and the ball is not just dropped in front of the thrower.

The throw-in will be awarded to the other team if the thrower ignores the referee's indication of where the throw should be taken from and takes the throw from a different position.

Goal kicks

A goal may be scored directly from a goal kick, but only against the opposing team.

Opponents must stay outside the penalty area until the ball passes out of the area and is in play.

The kicker may not play the ball a second time until it has touched another player.

A player cannot be offside from a goal kick.

Corner kicks

A goal may be scored directly from a corner kick, but only against the opposing team.

The kicker cannot play the ball a second time until it has touched another player. Referees have to watch that a ball doesn't rebound to the kicker off the goalpost as he can't kick it again.

For a corner kick there is no requirement for the ball to be placed wholly in the corner arc – only part of the ball has to be on the corner arc line or indeed inside it.

Figure 9 **Corner kick**

Penalty shoot outs

Quote | 'An incredibly exciting end to a game is when there are kicks from the penalty mark to decide the result.'

'Kicks from the penalty mark' is a procedure to ensure that a result of a match is determined on the day. It is highly emotional and one has to feel sorry for the player whose kick misses or is saved and whose team therefore loses.

Quote | 'There have been many notable occasions when the English team has been eliminated from competitions in this way.'

Fans often wonder how the decision is made concerning the end the kicks will be taken from. This can be an important decision if the supporters of one team are behind one goal and those of the other team are at the opposite goal. If there are no special security or pitch condition concerns the decision lies with the referee. In FA competitions The FA advises referees to toss a coin in front of the captains and say, 'If the coin comes down heads we will use the goal to my left, if it comes down tails we will use the goal to my right.' In this way the referee is determining the end but all is seen to be fair.

A toss of the coin determines which team starts the kicks from the penalty mark, the team that wins the toss has the choice of taking the first or second kick.

The first stage is to try to establish a winner after the first five kicks from each team. Sometimes it doesn't even go that far if a team falls behind and cannot catch up within the five kicks.

If the scores are still level after the ten kicks we go to 'sudden death'. This means that the teams continue to take kicks in turn until one team has scored more goals after both teams have taken an equal number of kicks.

Best Practice If your team is playing in a competition where a penalty shoot out could occur, make sure that the team has a plan in place for who will take the penalties. Only players who are on the field at full time can take a kick so if one of your best penalty takers is on the substitutes' bench make sure that he is on the pitch when the referee blows the full-time whistle or he will not be able to take a penalty.

Before the kicks begin all club officials leave the field and only the players are left. To make things fair in case additional kicks have to be taken in the 'sudden death' situation, it is important that the two teams have equal numbers before the kicks commence. If a team is reduced because of injury to or dismissal of any of its players, the other team stands down a number of players to make the numbers equal. If this were not the case the team with fewer players would return to their stronger kickers before the team who had more players.

All players eligible to take the kicks go to the centre circle. The goalkeepers move to the goal line to either defend the kick or wait for their turn.

When all the players in the team have taken a kick from the penalty mark they don't have to follow the same order in taking their second kicks.

A substitute who has not taken part in the match, including extra time where it is played, may not take part in kicks from the penalty mark, except to replace an injured goalkeeper.

The fourth official

In the professional game, you will have noticed the fourth official appearing in the technical area just before the end of the half and holding up a board with a number on it (see page 82). This is the minimum amount of time the referee has said that he is going to allow at the end of the half, for time lost.

More often than not the commentator will talk about 'injury time'. This is only one reason for time to be allowed. Let's just think about all the occasions for which time may be lost and therefore allowed at the end of each half:

Substitution

Substitution can take some time especially if the substitute is not ready when the coach requests a change. The referee also needs to be aware that substitutions towards the end of a game are often time-consuming measures – he will therefore stop his watch and allow for this time wasting.

Assessment of injury to players

Referees are not necessarily trained in recognizing serious injury. Referees should play safe and allow the injury to be assessed by the club physio.

Removal of injured players from the field of play for treatment

If stretchers are needed or support from other players, this can take some time for which the referee makes an allowance.

Wasting time

Sometimes players take their time over restarts. You may recall occasions when goalkeepers have taken their time over goal kicks or players have been indecisive over who will take a throw-in. Often, towards the end of a game, time is consumed by getting the player furthest away from the corner kick on the opposite side of the field to amble across and take the kick. An alert referee will stop his watch to compensate for this.

If these actions are excessive the referee may caution the player concerned for unsporting behaviour, as well as allowing for the time lost.

Any other cause

This can be for outside agents, e.g. a dog or spectators, entering the field of play and delaying play.

It is up to the referee to decide how much time is allowed. Rather than make 'a best guess' the referee stops his watch on each occasion and blows for time when 45 minutes show. Should there be any further stoppages in the time allowed this would be added after the expiry of the 45 minute period in either half of the game. That is why the announcement is always, 'A minimum of X minutes'. It is safer to blow for time when the ball is in a fairly neutral position in the centre of the field.

The next time you're at a match, try and estimate how much allowed time the referee will add at the end of each half.

Summary

- All games start with the kick-off, but during the match there are lots of ways that games are stopped and restarted.

- Free kicks can be either direct or indirect and mainly occur as a result of fouls outside the penalty area.

- During penalty kicks only the goalkeeper and the penalty taker should be inside the penalty area and penalty arc.

- The goalkeeper can only move sideways before the kick is taken.

- The movement of a throw-in must be continuous if the hands are to go past the 'vertical plane' and the player must not lift his feet from the ground.

- 'Injury time' takes into account much more than just injuries.

Self testers

1 When would the referee restart the game with a dropped ball?

2 What is the advantage to a team that wins the coin toss in a penalty shoot out?

3 What are the five aspects that a referee includes in the calculation of injury time?

Action plan

Many players waste good opportunities from 'set plays' (free kicks, corners and throw-ins) because they are performed incorrectly and not in accordance with the Laws. This chapter highlights the main reasons for this, so coaches should make sure that their players know the requirements for correct restarts.

Chapter 4

LEARNING

The referee's job

THIS CHAPTER WILL:
- Examine the authority and the power of the referee.
- Look at the duty of care the referee has to the players.
- Highlight the reason referees play an advantage in some situations.
- Stress the need for good communication between the referee and players.

The authority of the referee

Quote | 'The role of a referee is so much more than most spectators, players and coaches realize.'

It is the referee's duty to:

- **Enforce the Laws of the Game – using the correct punishment when necessary.**
- **Control the match in co-operation with the assistant referees and the fourth official, where there is one.**

- Check that the ball used meets the requirements of Law 2.

- Check the players' equipment. The referee has a duty of care to players to provide for their safety. Sometimes players have to remove articles that would put themselves or other players in danger.

- Act as timekeeper and keep a record of the match. Law 7 lists the reasons for allowing lost time at the end of each half. Time is also extended in either half to allow for a penalty kick to be taken.

- Punish the more serious offence when a player commits more than one offence at the same time. For example, at a throw-in, if a player handles the ball in playing it a second time before another player has played it the referee would award a direct free kick for handball not an indirect free kick for playing the ball a second time as handball is a more serious offence. It does not mean that if a player to be penalized for offside were tripped by an opponent the referee would penalize the trip because this is more serious. In this case, the referee would penalize the offside (the first offence) and speak severely to or caution the opponent for unsporting behaviour.

- Take advice from assistant referees over incidents that he has not seen. This should occur only if the assistant referees are in a better position than the referee to see what happened.

- Keep unauthorized people off the pitch. The referee decides when physios can come on to the field of play to assess injuries or treat injured players. Referees err on the side of caution here and arrange treatment as soon as possible.

- Make a match report highlighting any key incidents that occurred including cautions and dismissals.

The referee has the power to:

- Stop, suspend or terminate the match for any infringements of the Laws.

- Restart the match after it has been stopped. Often the referee gives a whistle signal. However, this is not always necessary. At a throw-in it is usual just to indicate the position for the throw-in. Often the referee just waves to the goalkeeper to signal for a goal kick to be taken.

- Stop, suspend or terminate the match because of outside interference of any kind – this could include spectator interference, or an animal straying on to the field.

- Stop the match if, in his opinion, a player is seriously injured. If possible an injured player is removed from the field of play. If there is doubt, the game is stopped for the player to receive treatment. This is essential if there is any cause for concern over a head injury, a player losing blood or if he may have broken a bone.

- Allow play to continue until the ball is out of play if in his opinion a player is only slightly injured.

- Instruct any player bleeding from a wound to leave the pitch. He must be satisfied that the bleeding has stopped before the player returns.

- Allow play to continue when the team against which an offence has been committed will benefit (advantage). The original offence can be punished if the anticipated advantage is not gained immediately.

- Caution and send off players for offences. Where there is an advantage, the referee carries out these punishments when the ball next goes out of play.

- Take action against team officials who fail to conduct themselves in a responsible manner. The referee may expel officials from the field of play and its immediate surrounds.

Quote | 'Referees receive most publicity for decisions involving sending offs and penalties, but this is just a small part of their job.'

Decisions of the referee

The decisions of the referee concerning facts connected with play are final. Facts connected with play shall include whether a goal is scored or not and the result of the match.

A referee may only change a decision that he realizes is incorrect or on the advice of an assistant referee, provided that play has not restarted.

Duty of care – treatment of injuries

A referee will always do his very best to protect players from harm but there may be occasions when things go wrong. As long as the referee has demonstrated that he has done everything possible to protect the safety of players the Laws of the Game protect him from subsequent action.

A referee has to be really careful in situations involving injury to players, especially on local pitches without trained medical staff. The advice is always to err on the side of caution. Care needs to be exercised before a seriously injured player is removed from the field of play. Referees must continue to be vigilant and accept the advice of those who are medically qualified or claim to have similar skills. There is a particular need for rapid assessment and action in cases of head injuries.

Best Practice Football is a contact sport, which means that accidents and injuries can happen. It should be a priority of every club to ensure that there is always an individual with at least basic first aid training present at a match. We strongly recommend that clubs should follow the advice promoted by The FA and encourage those involved with the club to attend a basic first aid training course. The County FA's FA Learning scheme runs a number of courses designed to give the learner the basic skills required in case of accidents occurring on the pitch.

Visit **www.TheFA.com**/FALearning to find out more information about first aid courses that take place in your area.

If a goalkeeper is injured it is quicker to allow him to be treated on the field. If another player is injured at the same time he may be treated on the field as well. In these circumstances the players do not have to go off the field after treatment.

In the case of a player returning after treatment to a bleeding injury, the fourth official, where appointed, may assist the referee in ensuring that bleeding has stopped. If there is blood on the player's clothing following the treatment this still constitutes a danger to other players with cuts or scratches and the offending garments should also be changed.

A club trainer or physiotherapist who has been guilty of misconduct should still be granted permission to enter the field of play to treat an injured player. However, a player sent from the field of play for misconduct cannot return to the field in any official capacity.

Drugs and alcohol

If a referee suspects a player is suffering from drug or alcohol abuse he should seek medical advice rather than make an accusation which may be difficult to prove. In such circumstances, the matter should be considered as a team responsibility and suitable attention be drawn to a club official, perhaps suggesting that a player was too ill to continue/participate or that he seemed to have a problem.

Advantage

The advantage clause is an important part of Law 5. The opportunity for a referee to allow play to continue if he feels the offended team may be able to take advantage of playing on is useful as it allows the game to flow. The referee has to believe it would be to the benefit of the team offended before he calls 'play on – advantage' and waves his arms forward to indicate he has seen a foul but is allowing play to continue.

If the team doesn't get an advantage (for example, the ball 'bobbles' awkwardly or the fouled player trips over his own feet or immediately loses his balance.) the referee can go back to the original offence and give the free kick. It is not the same as in other sports. In football the referee has to decide almost immediately if the advantage has been gained – or not.

Even if the referee has applied the advantage clause he should still deal with any misconduct he observed in the original offence when the ball next goes out of play. This causes confusion among spectators who may have forgotten the original offence by the time the ball goes out of play.

▓ The next time you see the referee allowing an advantage to take place look at the decision made to understand why it occurred.

The game is off!

Have you ever been to a game that had to be postponed, suspended or abandoned? This decision would have been made by the referee, sometimes on the advice of police at professional games. The decision will have been made after very careful consideration of all relevant factors. In some circumstances, it will be obvious that the game will not commence or restart. However, in the event of fog, hailstorms, floodlight failure, crowd intrusion or other similar situations, it may be possible to commence or continue the game after a suitable delay.

Pre-season friendlies

Clubs prepare for the season with friendly games. Referees are not permitted to adopt unapproved variations in the Laws of the Game in these matches (including the use of 'sin-bins' for punishment of misconduct). The punishment of cautions and dismissals must still apply when offences requiring these actions are committed. Life for the referee is sometimes made difficult by team officials requesting a substitution rather than sending off a player. Referees agreeing to this are putting themselves in line for disciplinary action instead of the offending player.

Preventative refereeing

The Laws of the Game must be applied correctly and consistently in all matches. Match officials are given special training that enables them to spot potential trouble before it actually arises. This is called preventative or pro-active rather than reactive refereeing, to ensure the safety and co-operation of players. Referees who are alert to 'hot spots' avoid many cautionable offences.

The game also benefits when referees adopt appropriate people-management and good inter-personal skills.

Signals by the referee

The signals used by referees have been approved by the International FA Board for use by registered referees of affiliated National Associations. The signals are simple, universally in use and well understood (see Appendix).

Good communication

Referees are not expected to explain or mime all offences leading to a decision but there are times when a simple gesture or word of guidance can aid communication. Anything a referee can do to promote greater understanding will gain him more respect and make life easier for himself and the players. The FA encourages subtle gestures, but the exaggerated miming of offences can lead to argument and confusion and should not be used.

The maximum measurements of a field of play are 130 yards (120 metres) long and 100 yards (90 metres) wide.

The decisions of the referee concerning facts connected with play are final.

Good communication between referee and player is very important.

All signals given by referees should be simple, clear and distinctive.

As penalties usually result in a goal, they are serious awards, yet a referee should not shy away from giving a penalty if the offence attracts it.

An indication by the referee of the point where a throw-in should be taken may help prevent a player from taking a throw-in improperly.

A call of 'play on – advantage' confirms to the player that the referee has not missed a foul, but has chosen to apply advantage.

Quote | 'Open and honest communication with the players helps to gain their respect and will often lead to an improved relationship and a greater understanding.'

An explanation might be helpful in generating a greater understanding between referee and players when the ball is deflected across a touchline after touching another player in its path.

All signals given by the referee should be simple, clear and distinctive. They should be designed to control the game efficiently and to ensure continuous play as far as is possible; they are intended essentially to indicate what the next action in the game should be, not principally to justify that action.

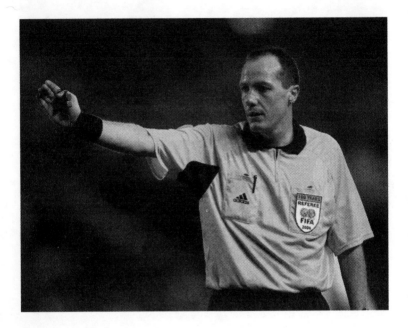

Agreed signals communicate efficiently

An arm pointing to indicate a corner kick, goal kick or foul, and the direction in which the kick is to be taken will normally be sufficient.

A raised arm to indicate that a free kick is indirect is clearly understood, but if a player queries politely whether the award is a direct free kick or an indirect free kick, a helpful word from the referee, in addition to the regular signal, will lead to a better understanding in future.

The proper use of the whistle, voice and hand signals by the referee and the flags by the assistant referees should all assist understanding through clear communication (see Appendix).

Summary

- **The referee has an extensive list of responsibilities that he must perform.**

- **The referee must always have the safety of the players as his key concern.**

- **Within the option of playing an 'advantage' the referee has the flexibility to call back play if the team benefiting from the decision do not gain an immediate advantage.**

- **Open and honest communication along with preventative refereeing is key to gaining the players' respect.**

Self testers

1 List the key duties of the referee.
2 List the powers of the referee.
3 Name some of the reasons why a game could be called off.

Action plan

Read through the powers and duties of the referee so that you understand just what is involved when refereeing a match. If you think that this is something you would like to take further then continue reading and then visit **www.TheFA.com**/FALearning for more information on refereeing and refereeing qualifications.

LEARNING

Chapter 5

The only team without supporters

THIS CHAPTER WILL:

- Look at the team of officials involved in football matches.
- Describe how the referee works with his assistants and the importance of co-operation.
- Detail the responsibilities of the assistant referees.
- Cover the signals the assistant referee should use as indicators for the referee.
- Explain the role of the fourth official.

Quote | 'It would be nice to be "loved" but we have to work at it.'

The team of match officials sets out to be the best team on the pitch. They are not always fully appreciated but this does not put them off.

Assistance

Assistant referees support referees. Early on in his career the referee will probably only be helped by assistant referees attached to each club. Sometimes they may even be the substitutes waiting their turn to play.

More experienced referees officiate in higher leagues and in later rounds of cup competitions and will be supported by assistant referees who are also referees in their own right. In these matches the referee can make greater use of his assistants as they are neutral and do not belong to one of the teams participating in the game.

The two assistant referees have specific duties to perform. They only indicate their opinion to the referee. It is important to remember that the referee always has the final decision, whether he is operating with club assistant referees or with neutral officials.

▓ When you next watch a match, look at how the referee relies on his assistants for support and to recommend what action to take. Are there instances when the referee overrules the assistants?

The duties of assistant referees, subject to the referee's decision, are to indicate:

• **When the whole of the ball has passed out of the field of play.**
Law 9 tells us that the ball is in play until it has fully crossed the touchline or goal line. In order to be sure that the whole of the ball has crossed the whole of the line, the assistant referees must take up a position that enables them to look right along the line. In the case of a goal line they must follow the ball down to the goal line to look right along it and give a correct decision.

• **Which side is entitled to a corner kick, goal kick or throw-in.**
Having decided which team is to be awarded a throw-in, the assistant points the flag in the direction that the team is playing.

To indicate the game should be restarted with a goal kick the assistant points to the goal area. If he thinks the award should be a corner kick he will point to the flag in the nearest corner arc.

- **When a player may be penalized for being in an offside position.**
  Law 11 (see Chapter 6) covers the conditions needed for being penalized for being in an offside position.

Best Practice Assistant referees should, whenever possible, keep in line with the second last defender (the last defender is usually the goalkeeper).

If the assistant referee sees a player in his opponents' half and in front of the ball and nearer the opponents' goal line than these two defenders he knows that the player is in an offside position. He will consider the conditions which would make it necessary to penalize the player(s) for being in this position before he signals to the referee.

He has to consider whether the player is involved in active play. The referee knows that to be involved in active play a player must interfere with play or an opponent or gain an advantage by being in that position. If he thinks the player is involved in active play the assistant will signal his opinion to the referee. If a referee allows a club assistant referee to assist in this duty he will need to check carefully during the game to be sure that the assistant isn't favouring his own team. Depending on the area you live in it may be that club assistant referees are not allowed to carry out this duty.

Check the rules in your league or competition to find out if assistant referees are allowed to signal for offside or not. If it is not allowed, is this rule adhered to at all times in your experience?

- **That a team wishes to make a substitution.**
  When a referee is busy he might not be aware that a team wishes to make a substitution. The assistant would therefore indicate this to the referee. Usually the assistant referee makes

his way to the centre line to supervise the substitution and ensure that everything is carried out according to Law 3. Sometimes, when there is a fourth official for the match, he is responsible for this instead (see page 82).

- **When they have seen something**
  It is not always possible for the referee to see everything, especially when things happen behind him or when players block his view. When misconduct or any other incident occurs out of the referee's view he can act on the opinion of an assistant referee if the assistant had a better view of the incident.

Club assistant referees can only perform duties in the first two bullet points on pages 72–3.

Assistant referees are meant to support the referee – they are not expected to be dominant and try to run the game from the touchline. They assist, as their name suggests, but the referee must remain in charge. The assistant referees simply assist the referee to control the match in accordance with the Laws of the Game.

Best Practice Assistant referees must remember that their job is solely to support and advise the referee when necessary. They have no power in their own right and must ensure that the referee maintains sole control of the match at all times.

If the referee is unhappy, either with the level of co-operation or the over-fussiness of the officials working with him, he can do something about it. Law 6 says that in the event of undue interference or improper conduct, the referee can relieve an assistant referee of his duties and make a report to the appropriate authorities. Naturally, the officials would first discuss what is happening and the referee would offer suggestions as to how things could be improved, but if things didn't improve the action indicated in the Law would be followed.

▓   When you next watch a match, study how the referee interacts with the assistants. If you can, compare the relationship of the referee and assistants officiating at an amateur match with those at a professional league game. Are there any specific differences in the relationship that you notice?

Signals by the assistant referee

When play has been stopped the assistant referee should assist the referee by signalling for the following incidents:

Offside

The assistant referee should lower his flag a full arm's length to indicate the position of the offending player. When the referee blows his whistle to stop the game the assistant points the flag downwards for players near

Figure 10 **Signalling offside**

him, straight across for players in the middle of the field and upwards for those at the far side.

Throw-in

When the ball goes out of play over the touchline on his side of the field, the assistant referee should indicate the direction of the throw. He should also signal if the thrower's feet, at the moment of release of the ball, are incorrectly placed. The correct action of the thrower is described in Chapter 1, page 22.

Corner and goal kicks

When the whole of the ball goes out of play over the goal line the assistant referee should indicate whether a corner kick or a goal kick should be given.

The normal signal for a goal kick is to point to the goal area line.

For a corner kick the assistant points to the corner arc nearest to him.

Best Practice It can help the referee if the assistant takes a few steps around the corner to emphasize the signal for a corner kick and turns his back to the goal line after signalling a goal kick.

Goal

When the referee indicates that a goal is scored the assistant referee should return quickly to his position towards the halfway line.

Clear view of offences

An assistant referee should advise the referee of any offence when he has a clearer view of the action. This will usually relate to an assistant referee who is close to play but may, in exceptional circumstances, be the assistant who is further from the action.

This will only be undertaken where the assistant referee is totally certain of what he has seen. The assistant will signal by raising his flag and holding it aloft until the referee sees it. Then the direction of the restart should be indicated. A pre-arranged signal, which should be subtle, may be used if the assistant needs to convey further information to the referee.

▓　Have you ever seen any other signals used by the assistant referees other than the ones covered in this chapter? If so, could you work out what was meant and why they were used?

Substitution

When a substitution is to be made, the assistant referee nearest the point of substitution should attract the attention of the referee by raising his flag and holding it in a horizontal position with the flag hanging down.

Best Practice It is important that the assistant does not obstruct his view of the referee with any signal he makes. This is particularly important for the substitution signal, which demands that the flag be held in front of him.

Figure 11 **Substitution**

Co-operation between referee and assistant referees

It is extremely important that the co-operation between the referee and his assistants is maintained at all times before, during, and after the game. This is especially so when the assistants working with the referee are attached to the clubs participating in the game. Listed below are guidelines that should be followed:

- All officials should be encouraged to maintain eye-to-eye contact with each other as much as is possible.

- Assistant referees must look for the referee whenever possible. It may be that a slight deflection of the ball is seen by the referee and he is able to give the assistant referee a discreet signal so that the correct indication is given in unison.

- All officials should remain focused on what is happening in front of them. Assistants cannot afford to be distracted by the crowd. They should never react to supporters' comments.

Best Practice When starting as a referee or as an assistant, it is difficult not to let supporters' (and players') comments affect you. It is something that you will have to deal with straightaway, so try to find the best way of handling such comments and criticism. As an assistant, it may be best to try to block out the crowd altogether, which, if you can achieve, will help strengthen your focus on the game.

- Assistants must concentrate on assisting, helping and supporting the referee at all times. They should not be too intrusive and should support the referee in every decision he makes.
- The assistants should try to identify how the referee is controlling the game, and match his involvement and empathize with what the referee is doing.
- At half-time any feedback shared between the referee and his assistants should be constructive and not destructive.

The role of the fourth official

A fourth official may be appointed under the competition rules. He assists the referee at all times. The competition organizer will determine what happens if the referee is unable to continue. According to seniority, the fourth official may take over as the match referee or the senior assistant referee may take over. If an assistant referee takes over, the fourth official would replace him as an assistant referee.

The fourth official assists with any administrative duties before, during and after the match, as required by the referee. He is responsible for assisting with substitution procedures during the match. He supervises the replacement footballs, where required. If the match ball has to be

Refereeing is a great way to keep fit – in an average match a referee can run up to 10 kilometres.

It is the referee's responsibility to check the goalposts, the markings and conditions of the pitch, and the ball before the start of the game.

A referee may only change a decision that he realizes is incorrect provided play has not restarted.

The role of the assistant referee is to support the referee and to try not to run the game from the touchline. They 'assist' as the name suggests but the referee must remain in charge.

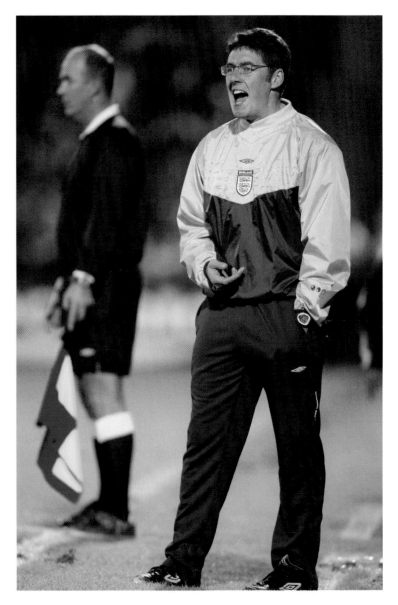

The referee is in control of all aspects of a game, this includes players, coaches, match officials and fans.

replaced, he provides another one, on the instruction of the referee, thus keeping the delay to a minimum.

The fourth official also has the authority to check the equipment of substitutes before they enter the field of play. If their equipment does not comply with the Laws of the Game, the fourth official would inform the referee.

If the referee makes a mistake and, through mistaken identity, goes to caution the wrong player, the fourth official would try to prevent this. It would be even more important if the player already had a caution recorded against him and this mistaken identity would have resulted in him being sent off for a second caution in the same match. Fourth officials should place themselves in a position so that they are constantly aware of what is happening in the game, especially as it is their responsibility to notify the referee of any instance when violent conduct occurs out of the view of the referee and assistant referees. The referee, however, retains the authority to decide on all points connected with play.

■ Have you ever seen a game where the wrong player was cautioned or sent off? How was this dealt with, if at all?

After the match, the fourth official must submit a report on incidents that occurred out of the view of the referee and the assistant referees. The fourth official must advise the referee and the assistants of what is in the report. He also has the authority to inform the referee of irresponsible behaviour by the coaches, substitutes or team officials in the technical area.

Summary

- Two assistant referees usually support the referee, and there can also be a fourth official present, especially in top professional matches.

- Assistant referees should support and assist the referee at all times.

- The referee is the only one who can make decisions. The assistants must remember this and that the referee is in charge of the game and relies on the assistants to help him.

- The assistant referees have specific duties to perform and use different signals to communicate what they have seen to the referee.

- The referee and the assistants should be aware of the necessity of co-operating and should work together to ensure the success and fairness of a match.

Self testers

1   How much of the ball has to cross the goal or touchline before it is out of play?
2   How does the assistant referee signal a corner kick?
3   List as many duties of the fourth official as you can.

Action plan

Co-operation between the referee and his assistants is very important and vital to the successful officiating of the game (see page 72). It does not always happen though and this can hinder the match. Think of the things you can do to help ensure the relationship is as good as it can be, and next time you are involved in a match, make sure that you carry out all the points you think of. Afterwards, review how each thing you did helped, what aspects of officiating benefited the most and, as a result, which points you will remember to do again at your next match.

LEARNING

Chapter 6

Offside ref!

THIS CHAPTER WILL:
- Explain the offside law.
- Describe what aspects of play have to be taken into account before offside is considered an offence.
- Detail how to restart the game after an offside offence has been committed.

Quote | 'There are more frequent arguments over offside than any other Laws in football.'

The Law regarding offside is relatively simple, but applying it correctly takes good skill, logical thought and good observation.

One difficulty a referee experiences is that in his earliest games he is invariably working on his own. At best, he will have two assistants attached to clubs. The two assistants may be substitutes waiting their turn to play, or friends and family of the players, anxious not to upset their friends or relatives. Very often, the first decision an inexperienced referee has to make is to decide whether to ask his club assistant referees to watch his own team's attacking players or the opposing team's attackers when making offside judgements. An assistant referee covers only half of the touchline keeping in line with the second last defender. Should the referee ask an assistant attached to a club to line up with his own team's defenders or with the opponents' defenders?

Quote | 'Many times I have heard, "It's easier to forget a wrong offside than an offside goal."'

For the reason given in the quote above, assistants attached to clubs are often asked to line up with their own defenders.

■ Find out about the local refereeing courses held in your area, and which one would be most suitable for you. Your local club will probably be the best place to start.

The law

The referee first has to decide if the player is in an offside position. You must realize that a player cannot be in an offside position in his own half of the field of play.

■ If a player is in an offside position, should he always be penalized?

The answer to the question above is important as a player should not always be penalized simply because he is in an offside position. For example, he may have received the ball directly from a goal kick, throw-in or corner kick.

Let's look at the Law logically and think first about what an offside position is.

Offside position

It is not an offence in itself to be in an offside position. There are certain criteria that must be met before it can be considered an offence.

A player is in an offside position if he is nearer to his opponents' goal line than both the ball and the second last opponent. In other words, if the player is 'behind the ball' in relation to his opponents' goal he is onside.

So, when a player takes the ball to the goal line and cuts it back for a colleague, the receiving player is onside as long as he stays 'behind the ball' or level with the ball.

A player is not in an offside position if he is in his own half of the field of play or level with the second last opponent.

This is why assistant referees always try to keep in line with the second last defender. This is also the position that a referee strives to maintain when refereeing on his own.

Figure 12 **Offside committed – the player is in front of the second last defender**

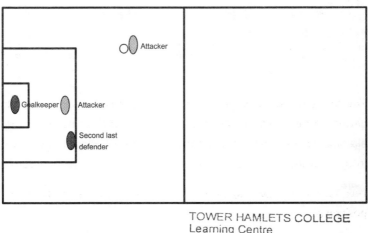

Figure 13 **No offside – the player is level with the second last defender as the ball is kicked forward**

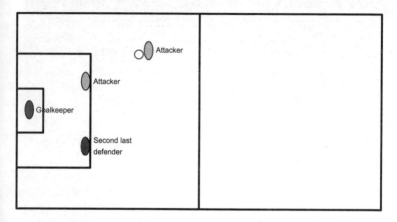

Let's suppose that the player is level with the last two opponents as the last two opponents may be in line with each other. So the referee first has to consider the attacker's position in relation to the ball, i.e. is the player in front of the ball? The referee then has to judge whether there are two opponents either level with the player or nearer to their own goal.

The referee must not forget to count the goalkeeper as one of the two defenders. However, if the goalkeeper has come out of his goal and is beyond the attacking player, there still needs to be two defenders level with, or nearer to, his goal than the attacker.

Having decided that a player is in an offside position the referee has to decide if an offside offence has been committed. If so, he would stop play and award an indirect free kick at the place the offence occurred or to be taken anywhere in the defenders' goal area if the offence occurred there.

Offside offence

A player is only penalized if he is in an offside position at the moment the ball touches or is played by one of his team.

Quote | 'Note the Law does not say when the player receives the ball, as is sometimes believed, especially by supporters of the defending team!'

The important point the referee must remember is to make the judgement on offside when the ball is last played by a team-mate. If the player is in an offside position at this time the referee will only stop play if the offending player is involved in active play. He would be guilty of this if:

- He got involved in the play by playing the ball.
- He got in the way of an opponent or obstructed the view of the goalkeeper.
- The ball came back to him from the goalkeeper or the goals and he gained an unfair advantage.

The IFAB has approved an interpretation of these three aspects of interfering with play:

How should we interpret 'interfering with play'?

- Playing or touching a ball passed or touched by a team-mate.

How should we interpret 'interfering with an opponent'?

- Preventing an opponent from playing or being able to play the ball, for example, by clearly obstructing the goalkeeper's line of vision or movements.
- Making a gesture or movement while standing in the path of the ball to deceive or distract an opponent.

How should we interpret 'gaining an advantage by being in that position'?

- Playing a ball that rebounds off a post or the crossbar having been in an offside position.

Figure 14 **Ball rebounding off an opponent**

The shot by a team-mate rebounds from the goalkeeper to number 8 who is penalized for being in an offside position because, when the ball is played, he is involved in active play and gains an advantage by being in that position.

- Playing a ball that rebounds off an opponent having been in an offside position.

No offence

Don't forget that there is no offside offence if a player receives the ball directly from:

- A goal kick.
- A throw-in.
- A corner kick.

Infringements/Sanctions

The referee needs to know what action to take and how to restart the game if a player in an offside position is guilty of an offence.

Summary

- There are different aspects to the offside law that must be taken into account before the referee can determine whether an offence has been committed.

- Only when the referee has decided whether a player was in an offside position, whether he was in this position when the ball was played or touched by a member of his team, and whether he was involved in active play, can a decision be made.

- An offside offence cannot be committed when a player is in his own half of the field of play or when a player receives the ball directly from a goal kick, corner kick, or throw-in.

Self testers

1 Where should assistant referees position themselves?

2 Is the goalkeeper counted as one of the two last defenders?

3 What should the referee award if he decides that an offside offence has been committed?

Action plan

Speak to those around you (friends, family, club members) about their thoughts on what the offside law is. It will be interesting to discover whether their views differ and if some people have picked up interpretations of the law that are incorrect. How much do they

know about the details and about taking into account whether a
player is involved in active play? Use what you have learned from
this chapter to help those who are unsure about offside become
more knowledgeable about the law.

Chapter 7

LEARNING

The referee must have seen that! – Fouls and misconduct

THIS CHAPTER WILL:
- Cover each foul or act of misconduct by players that might be committed in football and how each is punished.
- Look at the difference between the award of a direct free kick and an indirect free kick.
- Describe when the referee has to decide how the offence was committed, as this has a bearing on what is awarded to the opposing team and how the player is punished.

The game of football is meant to bring pleasure and enjoyment to all who play it. The Laws are written to ensure that play is fair and therefore have to be clear about what constitutes unfair play and how it will be discouraged through punishment.

Fouls and misconduct (Law 12)

Infringements of the Laws are punished firstly by awarding the restart to the opposing team, therefore punishing the offending team. Sometimes, the player who committed the offence is also punished by disciplinary action. Offences are treated differently, depending on their nature, and referees must know how each offence should be treated, and what punishments it attracts.

▓ Do you know how each offence should be treated, without reading the rest of this chapter? Supporters may often think the punishment given was unfair or harsh, but some offences attract certain punishments, regardless of the way they were committed.

Fouls and misconduct are penalized as follows.

Direct free kick

There are ten offences that are considered more serious than others and are penalized by a direct free kick or a penalty kick – depending on where they are committed on the field of play.

A direct free kick can be kicked straight into the opponents' goal, especially if within close proximity to the goal, and therefore it is a serious award, as is a penalty kick, which usually results in a goal.

The first six of the ten actions that are classed as penal offences give the referee the responsibility of judging the way the action was carried out as well as judging the action itself.

The referee has to decide if the player was:

- Simply careless.
- Reckless and taking no account of the opponent's safety.
- Performing the offence with an unnecessary amount of force and putting his opponent in danger.

Whichever manner (of the three described above) the referee decides the offence was carried out in he will award a direct free kick or a penalty kick. The referee may, however, decide to punish the player as well as the team with some disciplinary action. This will be covered in more detail later in the book (see Chapter 8, page 112).

A direct free kick is awarded to the opposing team if a player commits any of the following six offences in a manner considered by the referee to be careless, reckless or using excessive force:

- **Kicks or attempts to kick an opponent.**
  Remember that to attempt to kick, trip or strike an opponent is as serious as carrying it out successfully as far as the Law is concerned.

- **Trips or attempts to trip an opponent.**
  Referees watch for players tripping with the body by stooping in front of, or behind, an opponent to make the player fall over – often known as 'making a back'.

- **Jumps at an opponent.**
  Jumping for the ball is not an offence, but jumping at an opponent is – so the referee watches the action of the player to see if the player's eyes are on the ball or watching the opponent. Sometimes, players go in for a tackle jump at their opponent and put them at risk of serious injury from contact with their boots. Players may know this offence as 'going over the top of the ball'.

Best Practice The referee must watch carefully for players putting their opponents in danger by making contact with their boots and treat it as serious foul play (a sending-off offence).

- **Charges an opponent.**
  Physical contact through shoulder charges in safe areas of the body (the opponent's shoulder area) is still allowed, but careless or reckless charges with excessive force are not permitted.

- **Strikes or attempts to strike an opponent.**
  A goalkeeper who strikes an opponent with the ball or pushes the player with it should be penalized.

- **Pushes an opponent**.
  Pushing with the hands is fairly obvious and reasonably easy to spot. However players also push with their chests, hips and backs into opponents to push them away, and these are also considered offences.

The next four offences, detailed below, also result in the award of a direct free kick or a penalty kick. In these cases the referee simply has to decide whether or not they happened, rather than judging whether they were careless, reckless or committed with excessive force.

A direct free kick is awarded to the opposing team if a player commits any of the following four offences:

- **Tackles an opponent to gain possession of the ball, making contact with the opponent before touching the ball.**
  Players often shout, 'I got the ball ref!' but this is not the only consideration – the player must touch the ball before the opposing player, not after touching the player.

- **Holds an opponent.**
  Shirt holding is an example of this but players hold opponents with more than their hands.
  Referees should watch for the player standing on the boot of an opponent to prevent them from jumping for the ball. Players in a tangle on the ground sometimes trap their opponent's leg between their own to prevent the player getting up.
  A player can also hold an opponent by:

  - Holding out his arms to hold a player off.

  - Jumping with his arm over an opponent's shoulder to keep him down.

  - Using the opponent in front of him as a device to jump higher.

  - Deliberately blocking an opponent to prevent him going past him to get the ball or to get into a good position (we know this as a 'body check').

- **Spits at an opponent.**
  This is a disgusting offence. However, it must not be confused with players spitting on the ground.

- **Handles the ball deliberately (except for the goalkeeper within his own penalty area).**
  The referee must be sure that the offence was deliberate. He must watch to see if the ball struck the hand (no offence) or the hand struck the ball (offence). Sometimes a player will put up his hands to protect his face and sometimes this is understandable self-defence. Do not expect the referee to penalize simply because the player was advantaged by the ball hitting his arm.

Figure 15 **Deliberate handling**

An attacker, number 7, shoots the ball towards goal. Just before it crosses the goal line into goal a defender punches the ball over the bar. A penalty kick is awarded and the defender is sent off for denying the opposing team a goal.

If the referee is clear it was a deliberate act he may consider it unsporting behaviour if it was intended to rob an opponent of an advantage, such as a defender reaching up to catch a ball that he knew his opponent was going to run on to. Unsporting behaviour is a cautionable offence. When we look at sending-off offences later in the book we will come across handball again. This is because if the offence denied an opponent a goal or an obvious goal-scoring opportunity the offender is dismissed from the field of play.

The referee needs to know what action to take and how to restart the game. A direct free kick is taken from where the offence occurred. If the direct free kick is awarded to the defending team in his own goal area the kick can be taken from anywhere in the goal area.

Penalty kick

A penalty kick is awarded if any of the ten offences mentioned above are committed by a player inside his own penalty area, irrespective of the position of the ball, provided it is in play.

Best Practice Penalties are extremely serious awards as they usually result in a goal. The referee should be very careful in awarding them, although he should not shy away from giving a penalty if the offence attracts the award. Referees should seek the advice of the nearest assistant referee if appropriate.

Indirect free kick

In addition to the serious offences we have just considered, there are also some offences that are of a more technical nature. These are against the Law but are less serious in their potential for putting opponents in danger. They are penalized with an indirect free kick, which means that they cannot result in a goal to either team directly from the kick.

Offences committed by the goalkeeper

An indirect free kick is awarded to the opposing team if a goalkeeper, inside his own penalty area, commits any of the following four offences:

- **Takes more than six seconds while controlling the ball with his hands before releasing it from his possession.** The counting of seconds only begins when the goalkeeper is fully in control of the ball and his movements. However, if a goalkeeper jumps for the ball and takes steps on landing whilst regaining his balance, this time does not count. If a goalkeeper does not catch the ball but controls it with some other part of his body and dribbles the ball out to the edge of his area, this time does not count and he can pick the ball up in the area.

- **Touches the ball again with his hands after it has been released from his possession and has not touched any other player.**
  If the goalkeeper takes, say, two paces and puts the ball down to dribble it out, he cannot pick it up again until another player has touched it.

- **Touches the ball with his hands after it has been deliberately kicked to him by a team-mate.**
  This is often wrongly referred to as 'the back-pass'. The deliberate kick could actually be in any direction and would be penalized regardless of whether it was kicked 'back' to the goalkeeper. Non-deliberate kicks to the goalkeeper are not penalized. Sometimes a ball deflects from the defender to the goalkeeper, which is not an offence. On other occasions the kick goes back in the direction of the goal but the kick is not a deliberate one to the goalkeeper.

- **Touches the ball with his hands after he has received it directly from a throw-in taken by a team-mate.**

Next time you watch a match, study how the rule above affects the players and puts pressure on the goalkeeper. Does the goalkeeper make mistakes because of this?

Offences committed by players other than the goalkeeper

Players, other than the goalkeeper, can also be guilty of offences for which an indirect free kick is awarded. An indirect free kick is also awarded to the opposing team if a player, in the opinion of the referee:

* **Plays in a dangerous manner.**
  This puts other players in danger but does not usually involve direct contact. It could mean an overhead kick in a crowded goalmouth, or a player going into a challenge with his feet higher than is safe for an opponent.

* **Impedes the progress of an opponent.**
  A player who is not attempting to play the ball blocks the path of an opponent by standing in his way or running between the opponent and the ball.

> Quote | 'Do not confuse this with the player who keeps the ball in playing distance i.e. at any time the player could put his foot on the ball and play it, and he shields the ball from his opponent in order for it to run out of play. That is not an offence!'

You must remember that if the player makes physical contact in order to stop his opponent getting to the ball, this is 'holding' or 'body checking', which is penalized with a direct free kick.

* **Prevents the goalkeeper from releasing the ball from his hands.**
  The goalkeeper is punished for not releasing the ball quickly – but it is unfair to allow an attacker to delay the goalkeeper in releasing the ball.

- **Commits any other offence, not previously mentioned in Law 12, for which play is stopped to caution or dismiss a player.**
  If the referee has to stop play to caution a player, for example, for dissenting from the referee's decision, the restart would be an indirect free kick.

Infringements/Sanctions

The indirect free kick is taken from where the offence occurred. If the award is to the attacking team in the defenders' goal area the kick is taken from the nearest point on the goal area line that runs parallel to the goal line. The defending team would be allowed to line up on the goal line between the goalposts. If the award was to the defending team in their own goal area the kick can be taken from anywhere within the goal area.

Summary

- There are ten offences that can result in a direct free kick being awarded.

- Six of these offences also require the referee to decide the manner in which they were committed.

- The remaining four are punished however they were committed.

- Some offences are punished by awarding the opposing team an indirect free kick.

- The referee has to be very aware at all times to ensure he makes the correct award and punishment. This is particularly important as some awards can result in goals and the referee should always be sure that he has made the right and fair decision.

Self testers

1 What punishment is awarded if a goalkeeper takes more than six seconds while controlling the ball with his hands before releasing it from his possession?

2 If a player trips or attempts to trip an opponent, what punishment is awarded? Does the referee need to decide how the offence was committed?

3 What is the difference between a direct and an indirect free kick?

Action plan

When you next watch a televised match, take the opportunity to analyse how you would punish each offence, and what you would need to think about each time an offence is committed – you may soon realize that there is so much to consider that it is difficult to keep up. A referee's angle of vision will be different to the viewer's and he will, therefore, see things differently and make different decisions. Referees have to develop instinctive reactions and to be aware of many things at the same time. This is something that comes with experience, but in doing this exercise you can begin to understand just what is involved.

Chapter 8

Player management – control on the field of play

THIS CHAPTER WILL:
- Look at how to deal with players.
- Consider the use of red and yellow cards.
- Explain how to report misconduct after a game.

Quote | 'All club directors, managers and coaches, having the best interests of the game at heart, will know that a referee cannot be blamed for the bad behaviour of players.'

Referees are reminded of their duties in connection with breaches of the Laws. The relevant Football Association will support them in any steps that they may take to stamp out violent or unsporting behaviour.

Players should, therefore, be made to understand that acts of misconduct and displays of ill temper at referees' decisions will not be tolerated. The National Football Associations will deal severely with offenders.

Spirit of the game

The Laws of the Game and the decisions of the International FA Board cannot by themselves bring about an exemplary code of behaviour, which is often referred to as the 'spirit of the game'. If football is to continue to be one of the greatest and most popular games in the world, then those who take part in it must maintain its great tradition. Everyone wishes to win and there is often much temptation to win at all costs, but true sportspeople can find little satisfaction in victory won by unfair means.

Best Practice The 'Spirit of the Law' as well as the 'Letter of the Law' must be observed at all times.

It is permissible for a player to call instructions to a player on his own side during a game. This includes calling for the ball. Referees should only penalize such behaviour when it is done deliberately to deceive an opponent. The referee will stop the game to caution a player for unsporting behaviour, and then award an indirect free kick to the opponents.

How many times in your playing career did you appeal for a foul when an opponent called for the ball without indicating who he was calling to? 'Leave it' or 'my ball' was called and you cried, 'he didn't call a name ref and our players were put off by the call and left the ball for him'.

Disciplinary sanctions

The staircase of treatments – managing situations

As well as penalizing the offending team with a free kick to its opponents, the referee has to consider disciplining players who have committed offences. You will remember that one of the referee's duties is to enforce the Laws of the Game. If players are determined to break these Laws the referee has to consider how to bring them back into line.

The use of a loud whistle

This can be used effectively to let a player know that the referee has seen the offence and did not like what happened. Often a loud blast of the whistle communicates the referee's concern sufficiently.

A quiet, private word to the player

A referee will often run alongside a player after awarding a free kick to remind him of the offence and as a warning not to continue to offend.

A more public word of warning

This might be to either a team that is offending, when no particular player is committing all the offences, or to an individual player but in a loud enough voice to let players know the referee's tolerance is wearing thin and someone will be in trouble unless things improve.

Best Practice There is no need to work through this series of treatments if an offence is sufficiently bad to merit more serious disciplinary action. The more formal acts of discipline open to the referee are to caution or send players from the field of play.

Red and yellow cards

We are so used to seeing red and yellow cards used on the football field that we probably think that they were always part of the game. They were actually introduced by a famous English referee, Ken Aston, who thought of using them whilst sitting at a set of traffic lights in Kensington High Street in London in 1966. Here is how it happened in Ken's own words.

Ken Aston and the yellow and red cards

To caution a player properly was never a problem providing referee and players had a common language. I found it possible even if the player's language was strange to me by using a great deal of mime and gesture. Not all international referees used this method however. The language problem came to a head in the very important World Cup Final Series match in 1966 between England and Argentina at Wembley Stadium, refereed by Rudi Kreiltein who spoke only German. It was a difficult match not played in the best of spirits, and in the second half of the game he apparently sent the Argentine captain Rattin from the field. He didn't – and wouldn't – leave the field and after two or three minutes it seemed that Kreiltein would have little option but to abandon the match. This would have been catastrophic in such a competition. I had been appointed as being in charge of the referees generally and was seated on a pitch-side bench and felt that, even though it wasn't my job, someone had to do something to avoid disaster. I went on the field to Rattin and whilst I have no pretensions at speaking Spanish I had a reasonable understanding and a fair number of phrases in the language. Rattin said he wanted an interpretation and that he didn't know he had been sent off. I managed in the end to persuade him to leave and the match continued.

The following morning, a Sunday, the two brothers playing for England, Jack and Bobby (now Sir Bobby) Charlton were, as I understand, having breakfast in bed and reading the Sunday press reports on the game. Suddenly Jack exclaimed 'It says here I was cautioned. I didn't know I'd been booked, did you?' 'No' replied Bobby. 'It says the referee booked you as well' said the surprised Jack. So he rang Alf Ramsay on the hotel phone to find out what he knew. He didn't know that both Charlton brothers had been cautioned and rang FIFA Headquarters in the Kensington Palace Hotel. I happened to be in the office at the time when Helmut Kaser, the FIFA General Secretary, confirmed from the referee's report that the Charlton brothers had in fact been cautioned. I then left the office to drive home to see my wife Hilda for a few hours, having been away from home for some days. I drove up the small side street to the junction with the main thoroughfare Kensington High Street and the traffic lights fortunately were showing green. I speeded up a little to catch them before they changed – and at the last moment, they did! I then had quite a long wait till 'green' came up again, turned into the High Street where three sets of traffic signals about 50 yards apart were all 'green'. Just as I reached the first, up came 'yellow' followed by 'red'. Then the thought came into my head: 'yellow' – go carefully, take it easy!; 'red' – stop altogether! Thus the cards were born. As Deputy Chairman of the FIFA Referees' Committee, I was able to introduce them into the game at the World Cup Final Series in Mexico in 1970 – a World Cup distinguished by not one player being sent from the field!

Since that time, the use of the cards has spread not only through many sports but in other spheres also. They are used often in pubs in England for customers who become too noisy. The police in some places warn motorists by placing a yellow card on the car if it's parked in the wrong place. I have been told that the Speaker in the House in the New Zealand Parliament uses them! In conclusion, I have to say that I missed out seriously in the whole matter. Had I patented them at the time, I should have been a rich man – as it is, I haven't made a penny.

Best Practice Referees should not use either card in an aggressive or provocative manner likely to inflame an already emotive situation. Neither should the cards be used in an over-demonstrative manner, which may humiliate players and perhaps cause them to over-react.

Law 12 requires referees to use the red and yellow cards at all levels of the game. The mandatory use of the cards is merely a simple aid for better communication. A yellow card is used to caution the player, and if a player is shown two yellow cards in the same match he must also be shown the red card. A red card is used for a dismissal, unless that dismissal is for a 'second caution in the same match', in which case a yellow card will be shown immediately before the red card.

▨ It can happen that more than one player is sent off from a team during a match. Do you remember the minimum number of players a team can be left with (either through dismissal, injury or a mixture of both) before a match is abandoned?

Referees operating at international and some national levels have the option to show red and yellow cards immediately after offences or as above, so as to prevent retaliation and other reactions.

If a player commits either a cautionable or a sending-off offence during the half-time interval, he must also be shown the appropriate card(s) but, once the final whistle has been blown, similar offences will be treated as misconduct, reported as such and red or yellow cards must not be used.

If a named substitute commits an act of misconduct, he will be treated as a player, including being shown a yellow card or a red card depending on the offence. If this player is shown a yellow card, and at a later stage in the match commits a further cautionable offence, the player shall be sent from the field of play and shown a yellow card followed by a red card. This will apply even if the player is acting as an assistant referee on a local park's pitch.

Although the Law requires a referee to show a yellow card to a player as part of the cautioning procedure, failure to do so does not mean that a caution has not been administered and the player concerned will be dealt with in accordance with the laid-down disciplinary procedures.

After being sent off the player is expected to leave the playing area and is not allowed to sit on the trainers' bench.

At the end of a match, referees are occasionally drawn into unwise and unnecessarily prolonged discussions with club officials, managers, trainers, coaches and players, with regard to particular decisions or aspects of control. It is inappropriate for referees to become involved in detailed discussions at this time.

Best Practice Referees should avoid any discussions with members of either team following a match. It is the worst time to talk through any decisions made during the match, and members of each team may be angry and want to use the referee as a target for their anger.

Referees need to be careful that any comments made after the game to explain a decision to the press or club officials cannot be taken out of context and misinterpreted.

▓▓ When you next watch a televised football match notice the reactions from each team and how the commentators/ pundits will often concentrate on the negative aspects as they often command the most interest from viewers.

The FA is always anxious, however, to encourage the closest possible co-operation between club officials, managers, trainers, coaches, players and referees. Discussion between these various parties on aspects of the Laws of the Game and their interpretations can only be for the benefit of football, if they take place at more appropriate times.

Let's consider the offences for which the formal sanctions are designed.

Cautionable offences

A player is cautioned and shown the yellow card if he commits any of the following seven offences:

- **Unsporting behaviour.**
  This can be any act that is against the spirit of the game.
  If a player is guilty of an act punished by a direct free kick and

does it in a reckless way which robs an opponent of a clear advantage he may be cautioned.

- **Shows dissent by word or action.**
  It is not an offence to disagree with the referee or assistant – it is the showing of dissent either by the words said or the actions shown that earns the player the caution.

> **Quote** | 'Did you know that the showing of dissent against the assistant referee is also an offence? Usually this will only happen where there are neutral assistant referees.'

- **Persistently infringes the Laws of the Game.**
  If a player does not respond to the sanction of a free kick but continues to offend, the referee can use a caution to remind the player of his persistent offending and hope that will bring him back in line. Often when you see players cautioned for persistent infringement the referee will remind them of the warnings given at other times in the game.

  ▓ Study referees and their actions and words if possible when they are giving yellow cards to players. What do you notice? Do they remind the players of their persistent infringement if this is the cause of the yellow card?

- **Delays the restart of play**
  Players sometimes kick the ball away at throw-ins or keep the ball after a free kick is awarded. This is designed to delay play and give the offenders an unfair advantage. Some players prevent free kicks being taken quickly by standing over the ball or moving it.

- **Fails to respect the required distance when play is restarted with a corner kick or free kick.**
  Players in the defensive wall should be 10 yards (9.15 m) from the ball at free kicks. Refusing to retire to this distance or

Figure 16 **Failure to respect the required distance**

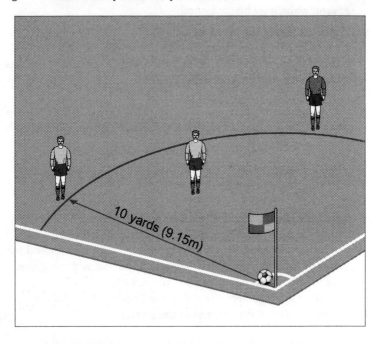

breaking early from the wall to intercept the ball before it has been kicked is a cautionable offence.

Similarly it is an offence if players delay corner kicks by failing to retire 10 yards (9.15 m). Most grounds now have the optional mark 10 yards (9.15 m) from the corner arc to tell the players how close they can be.

- **Enters or re-enters the field of play without the referee's permission.**
  Players joining the team late, coming back after equipment adjustment or injury, should seek the referee's permission to join or rejoin their team. Substitutes who come on without permission fall into this category.

- **Deliberately leaves the field of play without the referee's permission.**
Don't confuse this with accidental leaving of the field of play or stepping off to avoid being caught offside. This section of Law is designed to stop deliberate leaving of the field without the referee's permission.

Sending-off offences

A player is sent off and shown the red card if he commits any of the following seven offences:

- **Serious foul play.**
Any offence committed against an opponent that the referee considers could seriously endanger the safety of opponents.

- **Violent conduct.**
An act of violence committed against any person.

- **Spits at an opponent or any other person.**
Remember that spitting at an opponent is also an offence penalized by a direct free kick or penalty kick. Spitting at other people would result in an indirect free kick if play was stopped to send the player off.

- **Denies the opposing team a goal or an obvious goal-scoring opportunity by deliberately handling the ball.**
This does not apply to the goalkeeper within his own penalty area.

- **Denies an obvious goal-scoring opportunity to an opponent moving towards the player's goal by an offence punishable by a free kick or a penalty kick.**
Note the words 'obvious', and 'moving towards the player's goal'. If the offence was sufficiently serious but the goal-scoring opportunity was not obvious because the player was moving away from goal or there were other opponents nearby the referee would consider cautioning the offender.

- **Uses offensive, insulting or abusive language.**
Any language that causes offence falls into this category. Authorities are anxious to ensure that racial abuse is removed from football, and this should begin with the players.

Best Practice Referees should not tolerate any offensive language from players or any other official of the teams. Referees have the power to punish any such actions, and in doing so, help to achieve the aim of stamping out such offences in the game altogether.

- **Receives a second caution in the same match.**
  A second caution for any of the seven reasons given above.

The International FA Board's decisions

The IFAB also makes decisions that are designed to expand on the Laws and guide referees in their application.

The decisions of the IFAB in respect of Law 12 are:

1   A penalty kick is awarded if, while the ball is in play, the goalkeeper, inside his own penalty area, strikes or attempts to strike an opponent by throwing the ball at the player.

2   A player who commits a cautionable or sending-off offence, either on or off the field of play, whether directed towards an opponent, a team-mate, the referee, an assistant referee or any other person, is disciplined according to the nature of the offence committed.

3   The goalkeeper is considered to be in control of the ball by touching it with any part of his hands or arms. Possession of the ball includes the goalkeeper deliberately parrying the ball, but does not include the circumstances where, in the opinion of the referee, the ball rebounds accidentally from the goalkeeper, for example after he has made a save.

4   A tackle from behind, which endangers the safety of an opponent, must be sanctioned as serious foul play.

5   Any simulating action anywhere on the field, which is intended to deceive the referee, must be sanctioned as unsporting behaviour.

Reporting misconduct after a game is completed

One of the referee's responsibilities is to send in a report following the game, so that acts of misconduct can be recorded and punished by the footballing authorities.

In the referee's early games this will usually be the County FA or relevant authority in whose area the match is played. At higher levels the clubs are often registered directly with the National Football Association and reports will go direct to this organization.

Summary

- Referees should do all they can to ensure that all players and members of the team abide by the spirit of the game.

- The referee can manage situations in different ways depending on what has occurred.

- Yellow and red cards are key tools that the referee uses to control the game, and ensure the players act as they should and abide by the Laws.

- Yellow and red cards are very simple but extremely effective forms of communication between the referee and the players.

- There are certain offences that always attract cautions or dismissals, and the referee must follow the rules with regard to these.

- The referee is responsible for reporting misconduct to the relevant authority, and must do so after the match.

Self testers

1 What are the three main things that the referee can do to manage situations?

2 Name as many offences as you can that would attract a caution.

3 Suppose a player, moving towards the goal he is attacking and about to take a shot, has his progress impeded by a defender tugging his shirt and deliberately pulling the attacker over. What punishment should the defender receive?

Action plan

Take time to notice, at every match you watch, how the referee communicates with the players, and uses the different techniques described in this chapter. From analysing the reactions of the players to the referee's decisions and the referee's response, you will begin to develop an understanding of the most effective way of dealing with different situations.

LEARNING

Chapter 9

Why referee?

THIS CHAPTER WILL:
- Invite you to consider becoming a referee.
- Explore some of the misconceptions in understanding the laws.
- Help explain some of the instructions given to referees by the International Board.
- Stress the importance of fitness.

Quote | '30,000 people developing a hobby which gives them fresh air, exercise and a continuing involvement in the wonderful game can't be wrong – try refereeing and see.'

Refereeing is a very worthwhile and rewarding experience, and can provide a lifelong interest.

If you want to be a referee, ask yourself:

- **Do you love football?**
- **Do you want to put something back into the game?**
- **Do you want to be actively involved?**

If the answer to these questions is 'Yes', The FA would love to hear from you. Contact your local County FA whose number you will find in a local telephone directory. Or you could send an e-mail to newrefs@TheFA.com.

Every National Association has the overall responsibility for all football in that particular country, which includes the recruitment and training of referees. With thousands of football matches taking place every weekend and many more teams involved in small-sided games in leisure centres there is always a need for more referees.

Statistic
20,000 football matches take place every weekend in England.

There has never been a better time to take up the whistle. In most countries, you will gain information on how to become involved in refereeing from your National Association. In England, qualified FA Referee Instructors use modern training techniques to train all those interested in becoming referees. The FA produces videos and CD-ROMs to support referee training. For example, between the sessions of the course candidates have the opportunity to take home the CD-ROM 'Learn the Laws'. There are sections explaining each Law, video clips and animations for easy understanding and an assessment section to check knowledge. Many people use the assessment section first to find out just how much they already know.

Quote | 'We have all played so, of course, we know the Laws.'

Candidates are surprised how much they have to learn. We all have misconceptions that we picked up as children or spectators and have assumed to be accurate – until we start a course and learn what the Law actually says.

For example, how many of you have called 'foot up ref!' when an opposing player attempted to kick a high ball? The Law penalizes players for playing dangerously and it is true that a high kick close to an opponent could challenge his safety. But a high kick with no one around is fine. I am sure neither players nor spectators would like to see those magnificent goals scored with overhead scissor kicks outlawed. However, if the ball was followed into the net by an opponent's head, the referee might recognize that there was an element of danger that should have been penalized!

It is important that referees are offered support in their early games. In an increasing number of courses the new trainees are linked to mentors to offer help and advice in the transition from classroom to the pitch. The FA is encouraging this 'apprenticeship' approach to learning to try to reduce the number of referees who take courses but are put off in their early games by the demands of the practical experience of refereeing.

■   If you are interested in becoming a referee and taking part in a course, research what is available in your local area. You can do this by contacting your local or National Associations, leagues, clubs, or by searching on the internet.

Football is a team game and players enjoy the support, camaraderie and social contact with the rest of the team. If a player has a bad day there is always someone to encourage him to forget mistakes and not give up. At the beginning of their careers referees find themselves alone – they don't even have assistant referees for most of their games – and far from being encouraged not to give up, they are often advised to do so by the players, managers and spectators.

Mentors guide new referees through these difficult times. Often the mentor is not much more experienced than the referee he is helping and this is good because the difficult times are still fresh in his memory – so are the routes out of those difficulties.

Once qualified, referees are offered further training courses to help them continue to improve. We never stop learning and it is impossible to cram everything a referee needs to know into the initial training.

The written and oral examinations at the end of The FA course establish that the new referee has a good knowledge of the Laws and knows what to do in response to certain incidents in a game. However, the Laws of Association Football are very simple and leave a lot to 'the opinion of the referee'.

The importance of the referee's opinion

Look at the number of decisions that depend on how the referee sees a situation at the time, detailed in examples below. Consider the different interpretations and how they could affect what punishment is awarded.

Example 1 – Offside offence

A player in an offside position is only penalized if, at the moment the ball touches or is played by one of his team, he is, in the opinion of the referee, involved in active play by:

- Interfering with play.
- Interfering with an opponent.
- Gaining an advantage by being in that position.

Figure 17 **Offside offence**

The attacker is offside because he is involved in active play and is interfering with the goalkeeper by obstructing his line of vision or movements.

Being in an offside position is not an offence in itself. The referee (and assistant referees) have to use their judgement to decide if the player is involved in active play. Assistant referees are trained to wait and see whether or not the player is involved in active play before raising the flag. This appears to the supporter and commentator to be a 'late flag'. That is better than a good goal being wiped out because the assistant flagged just because a player was in an offside position, not because he was clearly committing an offside offence. Chapter 6 addresses offside decisions in greater detail.

Example 2 – Indirect free kick offences

An indirect free kick is awarded to the opposing team if a player, in the opinion of the referee:

- **Plays in a dangerous manner.**
- **Impedes the progress of an opponent.**
- **Prevents the goalkeeper from releasing the ball from his hands.**
- **Commits any other offence, not previously mentioned in Law 12, for which play is stopped to caution or dismiss a player.**

The referee has to decide each case on its merits and decide whether or not to penalize the player concerned.

Example 3 – Goalkeeper in possession

The goalkeeper is considered to be control of the ball by touching it with any part of his hands or arms. Possession of the ball includes the goalkeeper deliberately punching the ball and chasing after it, but does not include the circumstances where, in the opinion of the referee, the ball rebounds accidentally from the goalkeeper, for example, after he has made a save.

The goalkeeper has six seconds in which to release the ball from his hands into play so that another player can play it. Just when these six seconds start has to be determined by the referee. He will be looking to see that the goalkeeper has the ball under full control before counting the six seconds.

Example 4 – Deliberate tricks to circumvent the Law

Subject to the terms of Law 12, a player may pass the ball to his own goalkeeper using his head or chest or knee. If, however, in the opinion of the referee, a player uses a deliberate trick whilst the ball is in play in order to get round the Law, the player is guilty of unsporting behaviour. He is cautioned, shown the yellow card and an indirect free kick is awarded to the opposing team.

A player using a deliberate trick to circumvent the Law while he is taking a free kick is cautioned for unsporting behaviour and shown the yellow card.

Whenever a Law is changed to improve the game there is a natural temptation to seek out loopholes and defeat the change. The IFAB, the body given the responsibility for modifying the Laws and deciding on any disputed points, tried to improve the speed of the game by removing the opportunity for the defenders to deliberately kick the ball to their goalkeeper – the 'back-pass' rule as many people know it (see page 105).

In England the Law changes always come into effect on 1 July, preceding the new season. It became clear in practice matches and friendlies that the tricks to defeat the Law were being designed to counteract its effect, and the IFAB decision noted above had to be produced quickly to remove the opportunity for the tricks. The change of Law has been generally accepted and certainly speeds up the game. The tricks described are rarely carried out.

Example 5 – Instructions on celebrating goals

A player must be cautioned when, in the opinion of the referee:

- **He makes gestures which are provocative, derisory or inflammatory.**

- **He climbs on to a perimeter fence to celebrate a goal being scored.**

Leaving the field to celebrate a goal is not a cautionable offence in itself but it is essential that players return to the field as soon as possible. Referees are expected to act in a preventative mode and to exercise common sense in dealing with the celebration of a goal.

It is natural to wish to celebrate and there is no better occasion in football than when your team has scored a goal. That is what the game is all about and, contrary to common belief, referees are not 'kill joys'.

The instructions to referees, reproduced above, are designed to ensure that the celebrations are reasonable, and neither provoke bad reaction from the crowd and players nor put spectators in danger. There are many references to ensuring safety in the Laws and referees have to carry out these responsibilities without fear or favour.

Example 6 – Dealing with injured players

Referees must follow the instructions below when dealing with injured players:

- **Play is allowed to continue until the ball is out of play if a player is, in the referee's opinion, only slightly injured.**
- **Play is stopped if, in the referee's opinion, a player is seriously injured.**

None of us likes to see the game held up unnecessarily when a player rolls around on the ground as if seriously wounded or near to death, only to get up and run like a spring chicken when the 'magic sponge' or its modern day equivalent, has suddenly put everything right again. It is very difficult sometimes to differentiate between genuine injuries and play-acting. That responsibility is left to the referee who should only stop play if, in his opinion, the player is seriously injured. After assessing the situation the referee will call for an expert opinion from the player's physio or doctor and if the player can be moved the treatment should take place off the field of play and the game resumed.

Many spectators and commentators are genuinely confused by the need for a player treated on the field of play to be asked to leave the pitch until the game has restarted. The thinking behind this rule is, that had the player left the field of play for treatment, as the Law requires, the game would have been restarted and he would have been missing from play for the duration of his treatment. In order that the special privilege of treatment on the field of play is not abused the IFAB decided that players treated on the field of play would similarly leave the field for the restart. The game is often held up unnecessarily for treatment to a player very close to the goal line or touchline and to players who magically recover after minor treatment. It is this abuse of privilege that has brought about the instruction noted above.

How does the referee know when to penalize incidents?

Referees have to learn to use the knowledge they gain when training to develop an understanding of the Laws to decide when to penalize. This takes time and every new referee needs guidance.

The referee has to learn to:

- **See**: gain a good position on the field to have an uninterrupted view of the incident.
- **Recognize**: know whether a foul or misconduct has occurred.
- **Punish appropriately**: apply the correct sanction.

The instant response to situations only comes with practice and experience. Referee training always promotes discussion and, hopefully, learning for the next time. One of the most interesting training activities is to provide a group of trainees with four coloured cards. Red for a send off, yellow for a caution, blue for a free kick and green for no offence, play on. Incidents from real matches are then shown and a decision sought from all participants. A rainbow of colours results initially until referees become more skilled at recognizing offences and punishing appropriately. Participants are always left with the answer The FA recommends.

Figure 18 **Denying an obvious goal-scoring opportunity**

An attacker is moving towards goal with an obvious goal-scoring opportunity when he is tripped by a defender. The defender is sent off for denying an opponent an obvious goal-scoring opportunity.

Referee fitness

For the last few years referees operating at the highest level in England i.e. those refereeing in the FA Premier League have been given the opportunity to earn a living from refereeing. One of the greatest benefits coming from this is the improved level of physical fitness they display. The FA is trying to build on this success by raising the profile of the need for fitness in the minds of all referees.

Quote | 'Keep fit to referee, not referee to keep fit.'

Statistic
A referee can cover up to **10 kilometres** in a game.

The FA fully acknowledge that there are many referees who are making a tremendous contribution to the game but who are not seeking promotion to higher levels of refereeing. The FA know that for some of these people refereeing does keep them fit and contributes to an active lifestyle. We are really grateful for their dedication. Local football would be in a much poorer state without their dedicated service.

Advantages of becoming a referee

Finally, think about some of the advantages of becoming a referee:

* Lots of fresh air and exercise.
* Continued active involvement in the game you love.
* Enjoyment – yes you do have to put up with some moaning but most people recognize that the game would be poorer without referees.
* Money – small rewards at first but there are now 21 top referees in the UK making a living from what started out as a hobby.
* The 'refereeing family' is a close one. Involvement in the game is much longer than the active life of a player. Many friendships are formed which span a lifetime.
* In England, after a short course of instruction you can start out on your career as a referee. Any course costs you incur will be refunded once you have completed your first ten games. You will also become the proud owner of The FA's Three Lions badge to wear on your uniform. From then on you will receive the continuing support of mentors, fellow referees, your Regional Manager and the Referees' Committee of your local County FA. There has never been a better time to take up the whistle. Please consider this invitation. You will be made very welcome.

Summary

- There are many reasons for becoming involved in refereeing.

- Many refereeing decisions depend upon how the referee sees what happens at a particular time.

- The referee should use the 'See, Recognize, Punish appropriately' procedure.

Self testers

1 Approximately how many kilometres might a referee cover during a match?

2 Name three offences that would lead to an indirect free kick.

3 Approximately how many football matches take place every weekend?

Action plan

Give refereeing some thought and consider some of the benefits that have been covered in this chapter.

LEARNING

Conclusion

I hope you have enjoyed our trip through the Laws of the Game and the techniques that referees employ in order to maintain control over their games.

Football is 'the beautiful game' and most people agree that it is more beautiful when there is a referee in control.

Quote | 'The referee is an essential part of the modern game. There can never be too many referees!'

Statistic

In England, there is a national shortage of referees to cover sanctioned matches. The FA would welcome an increase of 20 per cent in recruitment to cover all games.

I hope that by developing an understanding of the role of the referee and the challenges he faces in doing his job effectively the referee's job will be made easier rather than harder. Too many referees give up because of the hassle they experience.

I believe that having a greater understanding of the Laws will enhance your own enjoyment of the game as a player, team official or spectator. I hope you find this to be true.

Before taking a referees' course you may like to test your knowledge and understanding of the Laws, and there are opportunities on **www.TheFA.com** website for you to do just that. In addition to this, the **www.FIFA.com** website contains the FIFA Question and Answer booklet online. This booklet makes available the decisions of the IFAB on situations that have actually arisen where solutions are required. The IFAB uses this document to communicate its interpretations of Law and rulings over incidents that have occurred in games.

You can become a referee from the age of 14, although you will not be allowed to referee adults until 16 years of age. The younger the referee starts the more chance he has of reaching the highest level. Many of the top referees started when young.

However, you should not get the idea that starting young is the only route possible as many players become referees after finishing their active careers. All referees have personal ambitions. For some it means gaining a place on the international list. Others look forward to continued involvement and an occasional local cup final.

Finally, this book is not a recruiting manual. Let me repeat my earlier message – anyone gaining a greater understanding of the Laws will increase their own enjoyment and appreciation of the game.

Appendix: Refereeing signals

Referee signals

Indirect Free Kick

Free Kick

Advantage
**Accompanied by calling
'Play on, advantage.'**

Assistant Referee signals

Substitution

Throw-in

Offside

Offside on near
side of the field

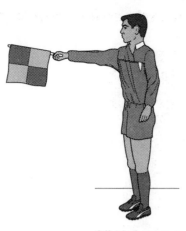

Offside in centre
of the field

Offside on far
side of the field

LEARNING

Contacts

Fédération Internationale de Football Association (FIFA)
FIFA House
Hitzigweg 11
PO Box 85
8030 Zurich
Switzerland
Tel: +41-43/222 7777
Fax: +41-43/222 7878
Internet: http://www.fifa.com

Confederations

Asian Football Confederation (AFC)
AFC House, Jalan 1/155B
Bukit Jalil
Kuala Lumpur 57000
Malaysia
Tel: +60-3/8994 3388
Fax: +60-3/8994 2689
Internet: http://www.footballasia.com

Confédération Africaine de Football (CAF)
3 Abdel Khalek Sarwat Street
El Hay El Motamayez
PO Box 23
6th October City
Egypt
Tel: +20-2/837 1000
Fax: +20-2/837 0006
Internet: http://www.cafonline.com

Confederation of North, Central American and Caribbean Association Football (CONCACAF)
Central American and Caribbean Association Football
725 Fifth Avenue, 17th Floor
New York, NY 10022
USA
Tel: +1-212/308 0044
Fax: +1-212/308 1851
Internet: http://www.concacaf.net

Confederación Sudamericana de Fútbol (CONMEBOL)
Autopista Aeropuerto Internacional y Leonismo Luqueño
Luque (Gran Asunción)
Paraguay
Tel: +595-21/645 781
Fax: +595-21/645 791
Internet: http://www.conmebol.com

Oceania Football Confederation (OFC)
Ericsson Stadium
12 Maurice Road
PO Box 62 586
Penrose
Auckland
New Zealand
Tel: +64-9/525 8161
Fax: +64-9/525 8164
Internet: http://www.oceaniafootball.com

Union European Football Association (UEFA)
Route de Genève 46
Nyon 1260
Switzerland
Tel: +41-22/994 4444
Fax: +41-22/994 4488
Internet: http://www.uefa.com

Associations

Argentina
Asociación del Fútbol Argentino (AFA)
Viamonte 1366/76
Buenos Aires 1053
Tel: ++54-11/4372 7900
Fax: ++54-11/4375 4410
Internet: http://www.afa.org.ar

Australia
Soccer Australia Limited (ASF)
Level 3
East Stand, Stadium Australia
Edwin Flack Avenue
Homebush NSW 2127
Tel: ++61-2/9739 5555
Fax: ++61-2/9739 5590
Internet: http://www.socceraustralia.com.au

Belgium
Union Royale Belge des Sociétés de Football Assocation (URBSFA/KBV)
145 Avenue Houba de Strooper
Bruxelles 1020
Tel: ++32-2/477 1211
Fax: ++32-2/478 2391
Internet: http://www.footbel.com

Brazil
Confederação Brasileira de Futebol (CBF)
Rua Victor Civita 66
Bloco 1 – Edifício 5 – 5 Andar
Barra da Tijuca
Rio de Janeiro 22775-040
Tel: ++55-21/3870 3610
Fax: ++55-21/3870 3612
Internet: http://www.cbfnews.com

Cameroon
Fédération Camerounaise de Football (FECAFOOT)
Case postale 1116
Yaoundé
Tel: ++237/221 0012
Fax: ++237/221 6662
Internet: http://www.cameroon.fifa.com

Canada
The Canadian Soccer Association (CSA)
Place Soccer Canada
237 Metcalfe Street
Ottawa ONT K2P 1R2
Tel: ++1-613/237 7678
Fax: ++1-613/237 1516
Internet: http://www.canadasoccer.com

Costa Rica
Federación Costarricense de Fútbol (FEDEFUTBOL)
Costado Norte Estatua León Cortés
San José 670-1000
Tel: ++506/222 1544
 Fax: ++506/255 2674
Internet: http://www.fedefutbol.com

Croatia
Croatian Football Federation (HNS)
Rusanova 13
Zagreb 10 000
Tel: ++385-1/236 1555
Fax: ++385-1/244 1501
Internet: http://www.hns-cff.hr

Czech Republic
Football Association of Czech Republic (CMFS)
Diskarska 100
Praha 6 16017
Tel: ++420-2/3302 9111
Fax: ++420-2/3335 3107
Internet: http://www.fotbal.cz

Denmark
Danish Football Association (DBU)
Idrættens Hus
Brøndby Stadion 20
Brøndby 2605
Tel: ++45-43/262 222
Fax: ++45-43/262 245
Internet: http://www.dbu.dk

England
The Football Association (The FA)
25 Soho Square
London W1D 4FA
Tel: ++44-207/745 4545
Fax: ++44-207/745 4546
Internet: http://www.TheFA.com

Finland
Suomen Palloliitto (SPL/FBF)
Urheilukatu 5
PO Box 191
Helsinki 00251
Tel: ++358-9/7421 51
Fax: ++358-9/7421 5200
Internet: http://www.palloliitto.fi

France
Fédération Française de Football (FFF)
60 Bis Avenue d'Iéna
Paris 75116
Tel: ++33-1/4431 7300
Fax: ++33-1/4720 8296
Internet: http://www.fff.fr

Germany
Deutscher Fussball-Bund (DFB)
Otto-Fleck-Schneise 6
Postfach 71 02 65
Frankfurt Am Main 60492
Tel: ++49-69/678 80
Fax: ++49-69/678 8266
Internet: http://www.dfb.de

Greece
Hellenic Football Federation (HFF)
137 Singrou Avenue
Nea Smirni
Athens 17121
Tel: ++30-210/930 6000
Fax: ++30-210/935 9666
Internet: http://www.epo.gr

Ireland Republic
The Football Association of Ireland (FAI)
80 Merrion Square, South
Dublin 2
Tel: ++353-1/676 6864
Fax: ++353-1/661 0931
Internet: http://www.fai.ie

Italy
Federazione Italiana Giuoco Calcio (FIGC)
Via Gregorio Allegri, 14
Roma 00198
Tel: ++39-06/84 911
Fax: ++39-06/84 912 526
Internet: http://www.figc.it

Japan
Japan Football Association (JFA)
JFA House
3-10-15, Hongo
Bunkyo-ku
Tokyo 113-0033
Tel: ++81-3/3830 2004
Fax: ++81-3/3830 2005
Internet: http://www.jfa.or.jp

Kenya
Kenya Football Federation (KFF)
PO Box 40234
Nairobi
Tel: ++254-2/608 422
Fax: ++254-2/249 855
Email: kff@todays.co.ke

Korea Republic
Korea Football Association (KFA)
1-131 Sinmunno, 2-ga
Jongno-Gu
Seoul 110-062
Tel: ++82-2/733 6764
Fax: ++82-2/735 2755
Internet: http://www.kfa.or.kr

Mexico
Federación Mexicana de Fútbol Asociación, A.C. (FMF)
Colima No. 373
Colonia Roma
Mexico, D.F. 06700
Tel: ++52-55/5241 0190
Fax: ++52-55/5241 0191
Internet: http://www.femexfut.org.mx

Netherlands
Koninklijke Nederlandse Voetbalbond (KNVB)
Woudenbergseweg 56–58
PO Box 515
Am Zeist 3700 AM
Tel: ++31-343/499 201
Fax: ++31-343/499 189
Internet: http://www.knvb.nl

Nigeria
Nigeria Football Association (NFA)
Plot 2033, Olusegun
Obasanjo Way, Zone 7, Wuse Abuja
PO Box 5101 Garki
Abuja
Tel: ++234-9/523 7326
Fax: ++234-9/523 7327
Email: nfa@microaccess.com

Northern Ireland
Irish Football Association Ltd. (IFA)
20 Windsor Avenue
Belfast BT9 6EE
Tel: ++44-28/9066 9458
Fax: ++44-28/9066 7620
Internet: http://www.irishfa.com

Paraguay
Asociación Paraguaya de Fútbol (APF)
Estadio de los Defensores del Chaco
Calle Mayor Martinez 1393
Asunción
Tel: ++595-21/480 120
Fax: ++595-21/480 124
Internet: http://www.apf.org.py

Poland
Polish Football Association (PZPN)
Polski Zwiazek Pilki Noznej
Miodowa 1
Warsaw 00-080
Tel: ++48-22/827 0914
Fax: ++48-22/827 0704
Internet: http://www.pzpn.pl

Portugal
Federação Portuguesa de Futebol (FPF)
Praça de Alegria, N. 25
PO Box 21.100
Lisbon 1250-004
Tel: ++351-21/325 2700
Fax: ++351-21/325 2780
Internet: http://www.fpf.pt

Romania
Romanian Football Federation (FRF)
House of Football
Str. Serg. Serbanica Vasile 12
Bucharest 73412
Tel: ++40-21/325 0678
Fax: ++40-21/325 0679
Internet: http://www.frf.ro

Russia
Football Union of Russia (RFU)
8 Luzhnetskaya Naberezhnaja
Moscow 119 992
Tel: ++7-095/201 1637
Fax: ++7-502/220 2037
Internet: http://www.rfs.ru

Scotland
The Scottish Football Association (SFA)
Hampden Park
Glasgow G42 9AY
Tel: ++44-141/616 6000
Fax: ++44-141/616 6001
Internet: http://www.scottishfa.co.uk

South Africa
South African Football Association (SAFA)
First National Bank Stadium
PO Box 910
Johannesburg 2000
Tel: ++27-11/494 3522
Fax: ++27-11/494 3013
Internet: http://www.safa.net

Spain

Real Federación Española de Fútbol (RFEF)
Ramon y Cajal, s/n
Apartado postale 385
Madrid 28230
Tel: ++34-91/495 9800
Fax: ++34-91/495 9801
Internet: http://www.rfef.es

Sweden

Svenska Fotbollförbundet (SVFF)
PO Box 1216
Solna 17 123
Tel: ++46-8/735 0900
Fax: ++46-8/735 0901
Internet: http://www.svenskfotboll.se

Switzerland

Schweizerischer Fussball-Verband (SFV/ASF)
Postfach
Bern 15 3000
Tel: ++41-31/950 8111
Fax: ++41-31/950 8181
Internet: http://www.football.ch

Tunisia

Fédération Tunisienne de Football (FTF)
Maison des Fédérations Sportives
Cité Olympique
Tunis 1003
Tel: ++216-71/233 303
Fax: ++216-71/767 929
Internet: http://www.ftf.org.tn

Turkey

Türkiye Futbol Federasyonu (TFF)
Konaklar Mah. Ihlamurlu Sok. 9
4. Levent
Istanbul 80620
Tel: ++90-212/282 7020
Fax: ++90-212/282 7015
Internet: http://www.tff.org

United States of America

US Soccer Federation (USSF)
US Soccer House
1801 S. Prairie Avenue
Chicago IL 60616
Tel: ++1-312/808 1300
Fax: ++1-312/808 1301
Internet: http://www.ussoccer.com

Uruguay

Asociación Uruguaya de Fútbol (AUF)
Guayabo 1531
Montevideo 11200
Tel: ++59-82/400 4814
Fax: ++59-82/409 0550
Internet: http://www.auf.org.uy

Wales

The Football Association of Wales, Ltd (FAW)
Plymouth Chambers
3 Westgate Street
Cardiff CF10 1DP
Tel: ++44-29/2037 2325
Fax: ++44-29/2034 3961
Internet: http://www.faw.org.uk

For details of County FAs please see **www.TheFA.com**/Grassroots

LEARNING

Index

All about FA Learning

FA Learning is the Educational Division of The FA and is responsible for the delivery, co-ordination and promotion of its extensive range of educational products and services. This includes all courses and resources for coaching, refereeing, psychology, sports science, medical exercise, child protection, crowd safety and teacher training.

The diverse interests of those involved in football ensures that FA Learning remains committed to providing resources and activities suitable for all individuals whatever their interests, experience or level of expertise.

Whether you're a Premier League Manager, sports psychologist or interested parent, our aim is to have courses and resources available that will improve your knowledge and understanding.

If you've enjoyed reading this book and found the content useful then why not take a look at FA Learning's website to find out the types of courses and additional resources available to help you continue your football development.

The website contains information on all the national courses and events managed by The FA as well as information on a number of online resources:

- **Psychology for Soccer Level 1 – Our first online qualification.**
- **Soccer Star – Free online coaching tool for young players.**
- **Soccer Parent – Free online course for parents.**

All these resources can be accessed at home from your own PC and are currently used by thousands of people across the world.

Psychology for Soccer Level 1

Enrol today and join hundreds of others around the world taking part in FA Learning's first ever online qualification.

This pioneering project is the first of its kind to be provided by any Football Governing Body and is available to anyone with access to the internet. There are no additional qualifications required to take part other than an interest in learning more about the needs of young players and an email address!

The course is aimed at coaches, parents and teachers of 7–12 year olds looking to gain an introduction to psychology and features modules based on 'true to life' player, coach and parent scenarios.

Psychology for Soccer Level 1 is a completely interactive, multimedia learning experience. Don't just take our word for it, read some of the comments from those that have already completed the course:

'Wow what a wonderful course! Thank you for the time and effort to make this possible.' **Tracy Scott**

'Just passed the final assessment … it was a good experience to learn this way and hopefully more qualifications will become available in this format. Thanks.' **Shayne Hall**

'I am a professional football coach working in schools and clubs and have travelled all around the world. I have really enjoyed the literature in this course and it has made me think about how I should address my coaching sessions. I want to progress in the field of sport psychology and this course has whetted my appetite for this subject.' **Chris Rafael Sabater**

The course modules are:

- Psychology and Soccer
- Motivation
- Learning and Acquiring skills
- Psychological Development
- Environment and Social Influences

In addition to the five course modules, learners also have access to a number of further benefits included as part of the course fee. The benefits include:

- Three months support from qualified FA tutors
- Classroom specific online discussion forums
- A global online discussion forum
- All successful students receive a FA Qualification in psychology

- An exclusive resource area containing over 100 articles and web links relating to coaching 7–12 year olds.

Within the five modules, there are over 20 sessions totaling over eight hours worth of content. Including the use of discussion forums, resource area and the course tasks, we anticipate the course will take on average 20 hours to complete.